Alexander the Great

Alexander the Great

Nigel Cawthorne

HAUS PUBLISHING · LONDON

First published in Great Britain in 2004 by
Haus Publishing Limited
26 Cadogan Court, Draycott Avenue
London SW3 3BX

A CIP catalogue record for this book is available from the British Library

ISBN 1-904341-56-X

Designed and typeset in Garamond and Futura by Andrea El-Akshar

Printed and bound by Graphicom in Vicenza, Italy

Front cover: CORBIS
Back cover: MARY EVANS PICTURE LIBRARY

Contents

The Man Who Would Be King
356 to 335

Alexander the Great was born in Pella, the ancient capital of the kingdom of Macedonia in northern Greece, in 356BC. The exact date is not known, but it was probably 20 or 26 July.[1] He was the son of the Macedonian king Philip II (382-336) and his queen Olympias (375-316). Later Alexander claimed to be the son of the supreme god Zeus or the Egyptian equivalent Ammon and mythological stories about his procreation and birth were invented.

It has often been maintained that Macedonia was a poor, backward country until Philip – its first powerful ruler – introduced civilisation. In fact, earlier kings had established cities, built roads and funded public enterprises with the proceeds of mining, and Greek artists – notably the playwright Euripides – had been invited to work in Macedonia. However, the other Greek states had traditionally considered the country backward because it was politically divided. The royal line was riven with intrigue, incest and murder. Philip himself was technically a usurper who had spent part of this youth in exile in Thebes, then a rival to Athens as Greece's leading city-state. Philip learnt his military skills in Thebes from the Theban general Epaminondas, who had destroyed the myth of Spartan military invincibility by beating the Spartans at the battle of Leuctra in 371.

Philip seized the throne of Macedonia in 359 after the violent death of his two older brothers. He quickly set about training a professional army organised along Theban lines, which Alexander would later inherit. The elite corps was the *Hetairoi*, or champions:

According to the Greek writer Plutarch of Chaeronea (46AD-c119), the night before Olympias consummated her marriage to Philip she dreamed that 'a thunderbolt fell upon her womb, which kindled a great fire, that broke into flames that travelled all about, and then was extinguished'. Philip, some time after his marriage to Olympias, dreamed that he sealed up his wife's body with a seal with the figure of a lion on it. Some diviners interpreted this as a warning, but the seer Aristander of Telmessus pointed out that it was unusual to seal up anything that was empty. He assured Philip that his dream meant the queen was pregnant with a boy who would one day prove as stout and courageous as a lion. It was also said that Philip later rejected Olympias when he found her sleeping with a snake. Being from the wild western fringes of Greece it was thought that she was involved in unusual – possibly orgiastic – religious practices.[2]

1,800 Macedonian noblemen, who fought on horseback. They were divided into eight units. One of these, the *Agema*, was the royal mounted bodyguard, which Alexander would later employ to great effect.

But the power of the Macedonian army came from the phalanx – six brigades, each of 1,500 highly trained infantrymen, packed in dense arrays in battle. They carried the *sarissa*, a pike six metres long, nearly half as long again as the standard Greek spear. Three 1,000-man units of *Hypaspistes*, or shield bearers, formed the royal bodyguard when the king fought on foot. The army was supported by a large number of military engineers for siege warfare, which would play an important part in Alexander's conquests.

After a year's training, Philip used his Theban-style army to win a decisive victory over the tribes in northwestern Macedonia, beating two rival claimants to his throne. He further strengthened his position by marrying Myrtale, the daughter of Neoptolemus, king of Epirus, the kingdom that lay to the west of Macedonia. She changed her name to Olympias after Philip's chariot won at the Olympic games in 356. That same year Alexander was born.[3]

While consolidating his rule elsewhere in Macedonia, Philip had ceded the Macedonian town of Amphipolis – with its gold and silver mines – to Athens. In 356, he took it back and struck his own coins, known as *philippeioi*, which bore the head of Apollo on one side and a two-horse chariot on the reverse. These have been found as far afield as Egypt, Sicily and Ukraine.

Despite its powerful navy, Athens found itself unable to retake Amphipolis. Indeed while the power of Philip's newly united Macedonia was on the rise, the rest of the Greek city-states were in decline. Sparta had lost the fertile plain of Messenia, its economic base, while Thebes was involved in fresh fighting, which drained its resources.

At the beginning of the 4th century BC, the regional power in the eastern Mediterranean was the Persian Empire, founded 150 years before by Cyrus the Great, whose conquests stretched from the Aegean Sea to the Indus. Cyrus's son Cambyses II took over Egypt in 525. Greece was little more than a collection of squabbling city-states, each with their own gods and system of government. Principal among them were Athens, Sparta and Thebes. In their periodic wars, they often sought the backing of the wealthy Persians, though they occasionally united to see off a Persian invasion. To the west, Rome was beginning to take over from the Etruscans in central Italy, while in North Africa the power of Carthage, near present-day Tunis, was still on the rise.

Although Athens had recovered from its defeat in 404 at the end of the long Peloponnesian War against Sparta, it was struggling to overcome some rebellious allies, who were turning to Persia for help. But Persian power itself was in decline. Several of its western satrapies, or provinces, revolted in 367-362 and it faced another civil war after 353, when Artabazus, the satrap or governor of Hellespontine Phrygia – the province that borders Greece – rebelled. This rebellion was eventually suppressed and Artabazus was exiled to Macedonia. But his rebellion had seriously weakened Persia's western border.

Alexander taming the wild horse Bucephalus

Alexander grew up in a country that was permanently at war and his father encouraged his interest in the military. He was a fast runner and legendary horseman. There is a famous story told of Alexander's horse Bucephalus: Philip bought the horse for his son for 13 talents, a lifetime's earnings for an ordinary man in those days. But when the king's grooms found the horse unmanageable, Philip told them to send it back. The eight-year-old Alexander, who had been watching their attempts to break it, said: *What an excellent horse they're losing for want of the skill and courage to master him!*

'So you think you know more about managing horses than your elders?' asked Philip.

Well, I could certainly deal with this horse better than they have, Alexander replied.

'All right then,' said Philip, 'if you try and fail what will you forfeit for your rashness?'

I will pay the whole price of the horse, said Alexander.[4]

Philip and his courtiers laughed. But Alexander had noticed that the horse was disturbed by the motion of the grooms' shadows, so he took him by the bridle and turned him towards the sun. When the animal was calm, he leapt onto his back. Bucephalus galloped off, but Alexander soon had him under control and cantered back with the horse now broken. Philip glowed with pride.

'You'll have to find another kingdom,' he told his son. 'Macedonia is not going to be big enough for you.'

Philip employed the philosopher and author Aristotle (384-322) to give Alexander a rounded education. This gave Alexander an interest in physics, meteorology, geography and theology. With Aristotle's encouragement, Alexander read the legendary poet Homer; for the rest of his life Alexander slept with a dagger and Aristotle's annotated copy of the *Iliad* under his pillow. Homer's poem is set during the ten-year-long siege of Troy by the Greeks. Alexander modelled himself on the central figure in the epic, the great Greek hero Achilles. Indeed, he claimed descent from Achilles through his mother Olympias. Through his father he claimed descent from Heracles, the son of Zeus and Alcmene, the granddaughter of Perseus, another of the sons of Zeus. So Alexander could claim descent from Zeus himself, the chief deity in the Greek pantheon. Later, Alexander would claim simply to be the son of Zeus or his Egyptian counterpart Ammon. His father Philip had also claimed divinity in his own right, erecting shrines to himself at Olympia, Ephesus and, it is thought, Delphi.[5]

Alexander also read the works of Herodotus of Halicarnassus (484-c425), known as both the 'father of history' and the 'father of lies', and the prominent general and author Xenophon (431-c350), who both wrote about the war between the Greeks and the Persians. He also learnt about Persia from Artabazus, the Persian satrap (provincial governor) of Hellespontine Phrygia,

who was living in exile in Macedonia, his children Phanabazus and Barsine, and by questioning visiting envoys from the Persian court.[6] Aristotle insisted that barbarian peoples – including the Persians – were slaves by nature and it was right for Greeks to rule over them.[7]

While Alexander was getting an education Philip greatly expanded his kingdom, adding the neighbouring states of Thrace, Chalcidice and Thessaly to his dominions. In 340, Philip went to besiege Byzantium – modern Istanbul – and left the 16-year-old Alexander on the throne of Macedonia, with the experienced officer Antipater as his aide. Alexander seized the opportunity to get practical experience in the art of warfare by putting down a rebellion of the Maedi people in recently conquered Thrace. He captured their principal city, turned it into a Macedonian military outpost and renamed it Alexandropolis. It was the first of many cities he would name after himself.

Although Alexander had proved himself in war both Philip and

The Persian or Achaemenid empire was founded by Cyrus the Great (c585-c529), who became king of Persis in 559 and defeated his overlord Astyages of Media. He expanded the old Median empire, campaigning in India and capturing Babylon in 539. Cyrus's son Cambyses succeeded his father in 530 and conquered Egypt in 525. Three years later, when civil war broke out, Darius I (550-486BC) took over and restored order. He founded Persepolis as his administrative capital and built a palace in Susa. Under Darius, the Persian empire grew to vast proportions, reaching from Macedonia in the west to Pakistan in the east, and from the Caucasus in the north to Libya in the south. This brought it once again into conflict with the Greek city-states on its western border.

Olympias were worried about his lack of sexual interest in women. It was the custom for Greek boys to find their youthful sexual outlet with other men, but Olympias feared that he might become girlish and effete. She begged him to have sex with women and even procured a beautiful courtesan named Callixeina for him.[8]

Philip was clearly intent on uniting Greece under Macedonian rule. The old city-states resisted, and in August 338, the Macedonians met the Athenians and Thebans in battle at Chaeronea in central Greece. It was a hard-fought battle and Philip was in danger of being killed or captured when Alexander led a charge that broke the line between the Athenians and the Thebans. Alexander showed great personal courage against the Theban elite, the Sacred Band. Of them, only 46 were captured. The remaining 254 died where they stood. The Thebans were butchered and over 1,000 Athenians were killed and 2,000 captured.[9]

Philip was now master of Greece. He was magnanimous in victory. He released the captured Athenians and returned the ashes of their dead. Alexander took them to Athens, making his first and only visit to the city. Philip then called representatives of all the Greek city-states to a meeting at Corinth. Sparta alone refused to attend. It was agreed that Greeks and Macedonians would no longer fight each other. Instead, they formed the so-called League of Corinth[10] and their armies, under Philip, would launch an all-out war on Persia in retaliation for Xerxes' attack on Greece almost a century-and-a-half before. In 337, war was formally declared.

Philip could not have picked a better moment. The Persian king Artaxerxes III Ochus had recently been poisoned by his eunuch the grand vizier Bagoas, who had replaced him with Artaxerxes' young son Artaxerxes IV, also know as Arses. Arses had yet to establish a firm grasp on the reigns of power and two Persian satrapies, Babylonia and Egypt, had revolted.

In the spring of 336, the League of Corinth sent an expeditionary force of 10,000 men, including 1,000 cavalry, across the Hellespont (the old name for the Dardanelles) into Asia. Led by Philip's trusted general Parmenio (c400-330) it was to liberate several of the Ionian Greek towns on the western shore of what is now Turkey. Then the news came that Arses had also been murdered by Bagoas. He was succeeded by a distant relative, Darius III, who in turn forced Bagoas to take poison.[11]

Back in Macedonia, Philip had decided to take a new wife,

In 546, the Persians had taken over the Greek city-states of Ionia in Anatolia, in modern-day Turkey. In 500, the Ionian Greeks revolted. The Athenians had sent a small fleet to support the rebels. Darius turned on them, landing 25,000 men near Marathon. Despite being outnumbered the Athenians won a decisive victory. Undeterred the Persians returned in even greater numbers ten years later under Darius's son Xerxes. The Greeks fell back to the narrow pass at Thermopylae, where the Spartan king Leonidas and 300 men faced a force of 200,000. Their suicidal action delayed the Persians for three days, enough time for Athens to be evacuated. The Persians pillaged the city, but the Athenian navy defeated the Persians at the battle of Salamis. Without ships to bring supplies, Xerxes was forced to withdraw.

Eurydice, the daughter of a Macedonian aristocrat. If she conceived a son, he would be a pure-blooded Macedonian, unlike Alexander, and a formidable rival to Alexander for the throne. Already there was tension between Alexander and his father as many people were saying that it was Alexander rather than Philip who had won the battle of Chaeronea.[12]

Rumours spread that Alexander might be illegitimate, encouraged by Philip himself, and Olympias was repudiated as an adulteress. She fled back to her native Epirus, where she stayed in the court of her brother Alexander, whom Philip had installed as king.

At the wedding feast for Philip and Eurydice, Alexander tactlessly remarked to his father: *When my mother remarries I'll invite you to her wedding.*

The Macedonians were legendary drinkers and things soon got out of hand. The bride's uncle, the brave and popular general Attalus, proposed a toast in which he 'called upon Macedonians to ask of the gods that from Philip and Eurydice there might be born a legitimate successor to the kingdom'.

Alexander leapt to his feet, threw a goblet of wine in Attalus' face and shouted: *Are you calling me a bastard?*

Philip drew his sword and lunged, not at Attalus who had insulted his son, but at Alexander himself. But Philip was lame from a wound and had lost an eye in battle. And he was drunk. As he lunged at Alexander, he tripped and fell crashing to the floor. Alexander stood over the sprawling Philip and said: *That, gentleman, is the man who's been preparing to cross from Europe to Asia and he can't even make it from one couch to the next.*[13]

Fearing his father's wrath, that night Alexander joined his mother over the border in Epirus. But the falling out between father and son did not last long. Philip could not afford to leave such a dangerous adversary behind in Greece when he marched into Asia and recalled Alexander to Pella.

Concerned about his prospects in Asia, Philip went to Delphi, on the slopes of Mount Parnassus, to consult the oracle. The oracle of Apollo at Delphi was the most famous oracle in the ancient world. The priestess there was a woman over 50, known as the Pythia. From as early as the 7th century BC, soldiers, statesmen and lawmakers from all over Greece would consult her in an attempt to discover the outcome of wars or various political actions. However, the answers she gave were usually ambiguous and wreathed in metaphor. Her response to Philip was typical: 'Wreathed is the bull, the end is near, the sacrificer is at hand.'[14]

To Philip, it seemed clear that the omens were good. Eurydice had just given birth to a son, whom Philip named Caranus after the mythical founder of the Macedonian dynasty, and he was about to head off on what he imagined would be an easy war. But first he hosted the wedding of his daughter Cleopatra to her uncle, Olympias's brother, King Alexander of Epirus. He elevated the wedding to a state occasion and, with representatives of all the Greek states on hand, again asserted his own divinity. However in the midst of the ceremony, Philip was stabbed to death by a young man named Pausanias. The assassin had horses waiting and almost got clean away, but as he ran towards them his foot caught on the stem of a vine and he fell. His pursuers caught up with him and he was killed.

Aristotle maintained that Pausanias killed Philip for personal revenge. According to the philosopher, Pausanias and Philip had been lovers. But when Philip dropped him for a younger man, Pausanias cursed him. Attalus exacted retribution by inviting Pausanias to a party, then having the other guests gang rape him. He was then left to Attalus's servants, who did the same. According to Aristotle, Pausanias took revenge for his appalling treatment.

However, Olympias's actions after Philip's death suggest a still murkier story. When Olympias returned to Macedonia after the death of Philip and found Pausanias still tied to a murderer's stake, she placed a golden crown on his head. A few days later she

Pausanias murders Alexander's father Philip

took the body down and burnt it over the remains of her dead husband. 'She built a mound there for Pausanias and saw that people offered yearly sacrifices at it . . . Under her maiden name, she dedicated to Apollo the sword with which Philip had been stabbed: all this was done so openly that she seemed to be afraid that the crime might not be agreed to have been her work.'[15] Olympias also had Eurydice, her son – Alexander's rival for the throne – and his baby sister murdered, it is said by pushing the children face down into a brazier.[16]

Alexander himself was implicated in the murder of his father. The men who pursued Pausanias and killed him were close friends of Alexander's. It is thought that they were co-conspirators who silenced the assassin after he had completed his job.[17] Afterwards, Alexander used the murder of his father as an excuse for a quick round of summary executions, which killed off his rivals for the throne, some of whom were backed by the Persian king Darius.[18]

With Philip dead, Antipater got the army to proclaim Alexander king and played a key role in the murder and exile of Alexander's rivals. He was rewarded with command of the Macedonian forces in Europe when Alexander went to Asia.

At this stage, it was crucial to get the support of Parmenio, commander of the expeditionary force in Asia. Parmenio was related to one of the rival candidates to the throne, Alexander's sworn enemy Attalus, who was Parmenio's son-in-law and was now with him in Asia. The pair had received overtures from Athens. The Athenians hoped that Attalus and Parmenio would turn against Alexander, weakening Macedonia and putting an end to its hegemony in Greece. However, sensing the danger, Alexander marched south. His army camped outside Athens and the city capitulated without a fight. Parmenio then threw his support behind Alexander and had Attalus murdered. However, Parmenio's price for his obedience was high. His relatives

At Corinth, Alexander was fêted by politicians and philosophers from all over Greece. But the philosopher Diogenes, who lived in Corinth, did not bother to come and pay his respects. When Alexander and his retinue sought him out, they found him sunbathing. Diogenes taught that happiness could only be attained by living as simply as possible; when Alexander delivered a grandiose speech of introduction, he did not even bother to get up or respond to the Macedonian king in any way. Embarrassed, Alexander asked Diogenes if there was anything he could do for him. Diogenes said there was. Could Alexander stand aside as he was blocking the sun? That was the end of the interview. Alexander's courtiers derided Diogenes, but Alexander was impressed. *If I were not Alexander*, he said, *I would be Diogenes*.[19]

retained key positions in the army, a hold that it took Alexander six years to break.

The Thessalians also tried to revolt, but were quickly called to order. Then Alexander organised a second conference at Corinth where Greek city-states were forced to reaffirm the treaty that they had made with Philip. Again Sparta declined on the grounds that, by tradition, its troops were not permitted to serve under a foreign leader.

After the meeting at Corinth Alexander headed off to see the Delphic oracle, but it was now late November. The Pythia did not work from November until mid-February and she refused to see Alexander. So he marched into the temple, seized her and dragged her into the shrine.

'Young man,' she said. 'You are invincible.'[20]

Alexander now made preparations to join Parmenio in Asia. But in the spring of 335, he found he had trouble closer to home. The Illyrians, who lived to the west of Macedonia, and the Thracian tribes, who lived to the north, revolted. Alexander immediately set out with a force of 15,000 men and, despite meeting fierce resistance, quickly put down the uprising.

But while this campaign was underway, the Greek cities to the south considered it the right moment to throw off the Macedonian yoke. The Athenian orator Demosthenes was particularly insulting, calling Alexander 'Margites' – the comic caricature of Achilles, a blustering coward, in a spoof of the *Iliad*. It was already well known that Alexander compared himself to Achilles. Demosthenes also spread the rumour that Alexander had been killed in the Illyrian campaign, even producing a man who pretended to be a bloody and bandaged messenger.

Greece rebelled, with the Thebans murdering the officers in the Macedonian garrison in Thebes. But Alexander was not dead. He rode south and, after a short siege, stormed Thebes. He razed the city, leaving only its temples and the house that had once belonged to the great lyric poet Pindar (518-438). Pindar had written an ode praising an earlier Macedonian king, also named Alexander. He had also propagated the cult of the Egyptian god Ammon (from whom Alexander later claimed descent), erecting a statue to Ammon and dedicating a poem to him.[21]

Philip II of Macedonia. Gold medallion, Bibliothèque Nationale, Paris

Alexander had 6,000 inhabitants of Thebes summarily executed and a further 30,000 were sold into slavery. But he treated the other Greek cities kindly and they quickly came to heel. He called a third meeting of the League of Corinth, which ratified Alexander's actions in the destruction of Thebes.

Although selling the Thebans into slavery raised some money for the Macedonian exchequer, Alexander had trouble paying his troops for the campaign against the Persian empire. Instead, he promised his followers crown land and its revenues if they followed him to Asia.

'But what will you have left for yourself, Alexander?' asked his army commander Perdiccas.

My hopes, was Alexander's famous answer.

All his commanders renounced their pay in the hope of a share in the wealth of Persia. For Alexander and his men the choice was now victory or penury.[22]

Cutting the Gordian Knot
334 to 333

While Alexander was fighting to consolidate his position in Greece, the tide had turned against the Greek expeditionary force in Asia. According to the Greek historian Diodorus of Sicily: 'Darius took warning and began to pay serious attention to his forces. He fitted out a large number of ships of war and assembled numerous strong armies, choosing at the same time his best commanders, among whom was Memnon of Rhodes, outstanding in courage and strategic grasp. The king gave him 5,000 mercenaries and ordered him to march to Cyzicus [in Turkey] and to try to get possession of it. With this force, accordingly, Memnon marched on across the range of Mount Ida.'[23]

Memnon of Rhodes and his mercenaries began to push back Parmenio. They launched a sudden attack on the city of Cyzicus and almost took it back from the Greeks, laying waste to the surrounding countryside and collecting a great deal of booty. Parmenio retaliated by taking the city of Grynium by storm and selling its inhabitants into slavery. Then he besieged Pitane, but Memnon appeared and the Macedonian army was forced to break off. Another force of Macedonians joined battle with Memnon in the Troad but was outnumbered and had to retreat onto the promontory of Rhoeteum, near Troy. From there, Alexander sent an appeal to Parmenio, telling him that Abydos, the last crossing point of the Hellespont in the Macedonian hands, must be held at all costs to maintain their lines of communication with Macedonia. Parmenio duly raced back to hold Abydos, thereby losing all his earlier conquests in Asia Minor.[24]

Parmenio was still hanging on in Asia when, in May 334, Alexander joined him with over 30,000 infantry, 12,000 of whom were Macedonians, and 4,500 cavalry, 1,800 Macedonians. The Persian force was now vastly outnumbered and Memnon thought they should avoid battle. He proposed that they adopt instead a scorched-earth policy, destroying crops, farms and feed for the Macedonian horses. At the same time, the Persian navy should go on the offensive, attacking Alexander's supply lines.

Alexander, who was already short of supplies, would be forced to return home. Although Memnon's proposed strategy was sound, he was not trusted. He was a Greek mercenary who had already rebelled once. Other Persian generals insisted it unacceptable to destroy Persians' farms and crops, and persuaded Darius to let them fight.

The Persians dug in on the banks of the river Granicus, the modern Biga Çay. If Alexander moved to the south to liberate the Ionian towns of Ephesus and Miletus, they could attack him from the rear. If he moved to the east directly against them, they believed that their position was strong enough to withstand the attack of a larger army.

Alexander decided to attack the Persians directly. But before he joined battle, Alexander visited

Memnon of Rhodes (c380-333) was a Greek mercenary leader and one of Alexander the Great's most formidable adversaries. Memnon joined the Persian ranks when his older brother Mentor (c385-340) became supreme commander in the West and married Barsine, the daughter of the satrap of Hellespontine Phrygia, Artabazus. After a failed rebellion against their Persian overlord Artaxerxes III Ochus in 353 or 352, Barsine and Memnon fled to Pella. Mentor joined the Egyptians but he soon betrayed them. In gratitude Artaxerxes pardoned him, his wife, her father and Memnon, who brought back valuable information from Macedonia. When Mentor died in 340, Memnon married Barsine, hoping to succeed him as supreme commander in the West, but successive Persian leaders did not trust the former rebel.

Troy, where he and his friend and lover Hephaestion took part in funeral games for the Homeric heroes Achilles and his friend Patroclus. They made sacrifices to Athena, poured a libation to the heroes and laid wreaths. At the tomb of Achilles, Alexander and Hephaestion anointed themselves with oil and raced naked around the vault in the traditional fashion. Alexander then recounted how lucky Achilles was to have had a faithful friend in Patroclus while he was alive and no less a poet than Homer to herald his fame after his death. He was asked whether he wanted to see the lyre of Paris, whose seduction of Helen had begun the Trojan War. Alexander refused, saying that Paris had used it to accompany *adulterous ditties such as captivate and bewitch the hearts of women*. Instead he said he wanted to see the lyre of Achilles, which he used to *sing the glorious deeds of brave heroes*.[25] Alexander also took a sacred shield from the Trojan temple of Athena, which later saved his life in India.

Then Alexander marched on the river Granicus where he found the Persians occupying strong defensive positions on the far bank of the river. Alexander wanted to attack straight away but, fearful of the terrible odds, his staff tried to raise religious objections. It was May, the Macedonian month of Daisios, when traditionally military campaigning was forbidden as men were needed to get the harvest in. Alexander made a quick adjustment to the calendar and declared that it was a second Artemisios – April II.[28] However, Parmenio persuaded him to delay his attack until the following morning.

The Persians always began their day with dawn sacrifices. This gave the Macedonians the opportunity to move downstream during the night and cross to the other bank in the morning, before the Persians were ready. Once Alexander's men were across the river, the situation had changed completely. The two armies now faced each other on a flat plain, perfect for Alexander's well-drilled army to manoeuvre on. The Persians knew that their infantry did not stand a chance against the Macedonian phalanx, so they launched a cavalry charge, hoping to outflank the Macedonians on the left and attack their rear. However, Parmenio thwarted the charge, while Alexander's archers and light infantry were sent against Memnon's Greek mercenaries on the right. This was the first step in a classic tactic of Alexander's, called 'stretching the line'. Typically, Alexander would make a diagonal attack from the centre against the enemy's flank. They would have to extend their line to avoid being outflanked but in doing so they would necessarily thin their defences. Alexander would look for weak points to appear – a gap opening up between units, say – then suddenly switch his attack there.

In this case, the ruse worked perfectly. The Persian line spread out to fend off his attack and Alexander then led his Companion Cavalry in a decisive charge against the weakened centre. There was a furious battle and Alexander was in the thick of it. Easily identified by his splendid armour and the large white plumes on his helmet, Alexander was attacked by two Persian commanders, Rhosaces and his brother Spithridates. Alexander's lance broke on Rhosaces's body armour, but he had

Hephaestion (c357-324) was a Macedonian nobleman and Alexander's closest friend. He met Alexander at school. During the campaign against Persia, Hephaestion sometimes served as aide-de-camp and later as a military commander. He is first mentioned in the literature when Alexander reached Troy in May 334.[26] While Alexander made his sacrifice at the tomb of Achilles, Hephaestion sacrificed to Achilles' friend Patroclus.[27] It was widely believed that these two legendary heroes had been lovers. The following year Alexander took a Persian mistress, Barsine (the wife of Memnon and before him his brother Mentor). Alexander was 23 and Hephaestion 24 or older; according to custom, by that age the time for homosexual love was over and a young man was expected to give up his male lover and marry. However, the friendship between the two men remained very close.

the presence of mind to jab the Persian in the face with the broken shaft. Meanwhile, Spithridates hit Alexander on the head with a battle-axe, chopping off one of his plumes and slicing through the helmet to the scalp. Spithridates was about to deliver the fatal blow when Alexander's Companion Cleitus ran him through with a spear, while Alexander finished off Rhosaces with a sword.[29]

With the death of Spithridates the Persian line broke and the Macedonian phalanx poured through. The Persian infantry fled. The Macedonians did not bother pursuing them. Instead they turned on the Greek mercenaries, slaughtering 3,000 to 4,000 where they stood. Another 2,000 surrendered and were sent back to Greece to be sold into slavery. Miraculously Memnon escaped.

Alexander moved quickly to liberate a number of Ionian

Alexander in the middle of the battle fought on the banks of the river Granicus against the Persians

Greek cities from Persian rule. The Persians had made use of the local aristocracy to run these towns and Alexander wanted to do the same. But he found he could not rely on this elite as they had previously sided with the Persians. Against his natural inclination, Alexander was compelled to establish democracies there – a political arrangement he discouraged back in Greece. In titular command, he left a satrap, usually a member of Parmenio's family promoted from the military, which had the useful effect of weakening Parmenio's grip on the army. As the elites in these new acquisitions could not be trusted, the satraps had no alternative but to enlist the support of the people. These new satraps were also supplied with finance officers who were loyal to Alexander and made sure that tax revenues were paid directly to him.

The liberated cities were garrisoned by Greek troops. Alexander had little time for these Greeks. His Macedonians did most of the fighting. He had brought Greek troops along with him largely as hostages to ensure the good behaviour of their home states while he was away. He now used them to hold the ground he had captured and maintain his lines of communication.

After the Macedonian victory at the river Granicus, Dascylium, the capital of Hellespontine Phrygia, fell to Parmenio without a fight, according to the written sources,[30] though there is considerable archaeological evidence that it put up a struggle. Alexander received the surrender of Sardis, the capital of the wealthy satrapy of Lydia. This allowed him to pay his troops. He then marched on Miletus, the largest Greek city on the eastern shore of the Aegean Sea, with an excellent harbour.

Darius now saw that Memnon's scorched-earth strategy had been right and appointed him supreme commander. Under Memnon's command, the Persian navy moved into the Aegean Sea from its bases in Egypt, Phoenicia (modern Lebanon) and Cyprus. The governor of Miletus was about to surrender to Alexander, but changed his mind when he heard that 400 Persian ships were on their way.

Alexander's admiral, Parmenio's brother Nicanor, took 160 ships and occupied the small island of Lade that commanded the entrance to the harbour at Miletus. His defensive position was superb: when the Persian navy turned up three days later, it was forced to anchor off Cape Mycale, too far from Miletus to help, but close enough to see Alexander's siege engines breaching the city walls. Once Miletus had fallen, the Persian navy sailed south to Halicarnassus (modern Bodrum, Turkey) the capital of the satrapy of Caria. Alexander besieged Halicarnassus, taking it after fierce fighting. Control over Halicarnassus was in dispute so Alexander installed Queen Ada, one of the rivals for the throne, as ruler. In return, she adopted him as her son and successor.[31]

Alexander then had to wait for reinforcements, giving the Persians the opportunity to regroup. Memnon planned first to retake the Aegean islands and he began by besieging the town of Mytilene on Lesbos. He contacted the Spartan king Agis, who was ready to rise in revolt against Alexander the moment Memnon gave the word. Athens was also eager to free Greece from Macedonian rule and readied a fleet of 400 triremes – fast, light warships armed with a bronze-clad ram on the prow and powered by three tiers of oarsmen – to come to Memnon's aid. Alexander's expeditionary force was now in clear danger. If its supply lines were cut off at the Hellespont, he would not only fail in Asia but also run the risk of losing Greece – and Macedonia.

With typical audacity, instead of turning back to secure his rear, Alexander marched on with the aim of taking the ports of southern Anatolia, denying them to the Persian navy. One by one, he took the ports of the provinces of Lycia and Pamphylia. None of these was as well fortified as Halicarnassus, and a show of strength was usually sufficient to force them in surrender. At the town of Hyparna, the Macedonians used the simple device of sending into the acropolis a group of dancing girls whose slave-attendants had daggers concealed in their flutes and small shields in their baskets. When the entertainment was at its height and the wine was flowing freely, the knives came out and the garrison was massacred.[32]

As Alexander's men marched along the coast, it was recorded that the waters in the bays seemed to recede to let them pass. Alexander's court historian Callisthenes of Olynthus – Aristotle's nephew – said the very sea had recognised Alexander's presence and withdrew as an act of obeisance. It was the first step towards making Alexander a god.[33]

With the ports under his control, Alexander turned inland to take the Anatolian highland and the satrapy of Phrygia. The country there was fertile and would provide grain for Alexander's men and fodder for his horses. The plains were also well suited to cavalry. If Alexander was to face Darius's army again, it was better to fight there than on the coastal strip. That winter Alexander invaded central Turkey from the south, while Parmenio invaded Phrygia from Sardis in the west. The two forces met in April 333 at Gordium, the capital of Phrygia, 50 miles west of Turkey's modern capital Ankara.

Alexander delayed there for some time, not wishing to travel too far east with the situation in Greece still threatening and Memnon's fleet menacing the Hellespont. He sent word to

The Gordian knot could only be untied by the future conqueror of Asia

Antipater, his regent in Macedonia, to assemble a new navy to defend the supply lines. Alexander awaited the harvest – taking it would have the double advantage of feeding his men and starving the enemy – and more reinforcements. His losses at Halicarnassus had been high and 1,000 Greek and 3,000 Macedonian troops were on their way. During Alexander's campaigns, Macedonian casualties were so high that his kingdom was drained of manpower. It never recovered.

At Gordium there was an ancient wagon dedicated to Gordius – the legendary founder of the city – by his son the Phrygian king Midas (718-695). Its yoke was lashed to a pole with an intricate knot whose ends were hidden. This was the legendary Gordian knot. According to legend it could only be loosed by the future conqueror of Asia. Always fond of oracles and divine portents, Alexander tried his hand at untying it. When he failed, he drew his sword and sliced it in two. In another version of the story he pulled the pole out of the knot, revealing its ends.[34] That night the sky was filled with thunder and lightning which the local oracles took to be Zeus expressing his approval, though it could

equally have been seen as an expression of his wrath.[35] However, for Alexander and his men, it proved to be a good omen. Soon after, news came that Memnon had died – seemingly of natural causes. Darius appointed Memnon's brother-in-law Pharnabazus as his successor. Alexander knew Pharnabazus when he had been exiled in Macedonia. He was not Memnon's equal and Alexander felt free to continue his march to the east.

Alexander left his one-eyed general Antigonus in charge in Phrygia, who set about subduing the tribes to the north and securing Alexander's rear. In July, well prepared and well provisioned, Alexander set off along the Royal Road, which ran from the Aegean across Anatolia to the Persian capitals of Susa and Persepolis. Although it was not metalled (covered with the broken stone or crushed rock used in road construction), it was probably the best road the Macedonian and Greek soldiers had ever seen. Once they had passed Ankara and entered the satrapy of Cappadocia, they turned south towards Cilicia and its capital Tarsus.

Alexander knew what lay ahead. In 401, a large number of Greek mercenaries had marched to Babylonia that way and one of their commanders, Xenophon, had described the journey in a book called *Anabasis*. Alexander knew that they would have to pass through the Cilician gates, a narrow mountain pass flanked by cliffs in what is now the Taurus Mountains. It was only just wide enough for two camels to pass. If the Persians had made a stand there in force, Alexander would have had to turn back. But with Memnon dead, the Persian generals now adopted his scorched-earth policy. They left only a small party to defend the Cilician gates while they burnt the crops and pastures on the plain beyond.

Alexander led a night attack with light infantry and archers, and forced his way through. Then he raced on to Tarsus, arriving just in time to prevent the Persians destroying it. He received news that Darius had recalled the Greek mercenaries serving with the Persian navy in the Aegean so reducing the threat to Alexander's supply lines. However, these mercenaries had been recalled to swell the ranks of Darius's huge army that was approaching from Babylonia. In his *Life of Alexander*, Plutarch says that Darius's army numbered 600,000 men. This is thought to be a gross exaggeration, but even a tenth of that number would have given Darius's forces an overwhelming superiority.

This time Darius, the 'Great King' of Persia, led the army in person. He was a demi-god, the ruler of the world. He could not be allowed to be killed or fall into enemy hands. His war tent was crowned by the image of the sun enclosed in a crystal, the symbol of Mithra – later Mithras in the Roman pantheon. He was the manifestation of the Sun, the lord of light and the god of just battles. Outside his tent golden trumpets sounded to mark the dawn. As his army marched westwards, it was led by a holy fire on silver altars tended by Zoroastrian priests, the magi, singing hymns and followed by 365 robed youths. Next came the empty chariot of Ahura Mazda, the supreme god, pulled by white horses and driven by men in robes of white and gold, followed by a great white horse sacred to the Sun. Next came ten chariots embossed with gold and silver, carrying guards of 12 nations of the Persian empire, each with their own weapons and dress. The elite regiments followed them. Then came the Great King in his chariot carrying embossed images of the gods in gold and silver. He wore a cloak decorated with golden hawks, the divine bird of legend. With him was the royal standard, always carried with the Great King both in war and peace. Darius also carried the symbol of the Tree of Life.

As Darius advanced Alexander lingered at Tarsus. Darius believed this to be a sign of cowardice, but, in fact, Alexander had fallen ill. He had been bathing in the icy waters of the river Cydnus – now called the Tersus-Tchai – that ran through the city when he was struck by cramps so severe he appeared to suffer some sort of convulsion. When his companions pulled him out of the water he was barely conscious. For days afterwards he lay help-less. He had a bronchial infection which turned to pneumonia and most doctors would not dare treat him. Certain that he would die, they were frightened of being accused of negligence, or, worse, murder. Darius had already offered a reward of 1,000 talents to anyone who killed Alexander.

However, Philip of Acarnania, a doctor who had known Alexander since childhood, volunteered to treat him. He told Alexander that there were certain quick-acting drugs that might cure him, but they were dangerous, possibly lethal. Alexander told him to prepare a draught. Parmenio had already written to Alexander warning him that Darius had offered Philip a great sum of money and the hand of his daughter in marriage to kill him. Alexander gave Philip the letter to read while he took the potion.

'When [Alexander] had perused the letter, he put it under his pillow, without showing it so much as to any of his most intimate friends, and when Philip came in with the potion, he took it with great cheerfulness and assurance, giving him meantime the letter to read. This was a spectacle well worth being present at, to see Alexander take the draught and Philip read the letter at the same time, and then turn and look upon one another, but with different senti-ments; for Alexander's looks were cheerful and open, to show his kind-ness to and confidence in his physi-cian, while the other was full of sur-prise and alarm at the accusation, appealing to the gods to witness his innocence, sometimes lifting up his hands to heaven, and then throwing himself down by the bedside, and beseeching Alexander to lay aside all fear, and follow his directions without apprehension. For the medicine at first worked so strongly as to drive, so to say, the vital forces into the inte-rior; he lost his speech, and falling into a swoon, had scarce any sense or pulse left. However in no long time, by Philip's means, his health and strength returned, and he showed himself in public to the Macedonians, who were in continual fear and dejec-tion until they saw him abroad again.'

PLUTARCH OF CHAERONEA[36]

The powerful draft had a dire effect on Alexander and he lapsed into a coma. But soon the crisis passed and, after three days, he recovered. Immediately he launched into a new campaign against the mountain tribes of Cilicia, lest they might close the Cilician gates behind him. Meanwhile Parmenio and a small army were sent to occupy the Assyrian gates. This pass lay between the coastal plain of Cilicia and the plain of the river Orontes, where the main road continued onwards from Cilicia to Babylonia. Alexander was convinced that Darius would come this way.

Parmenio received word that Darius's army was at Sochi, only two days away, and sent a courier to Alexander, who had taken Issus and was 75 miles away at the coast near Myriandrus. Alexander drew up plans to attack Darius in Sochi, only to discover that he was no longer there. The Persian army had made a quick dash through the Amanic gates and retaken Issus, where Alexander had left his wounded, thinking they would be safe. The Persians cut off the hands of Alexander's wounded men and sealed the stumps with hot pitch. Then Darius showed them his huge army and sent them to Alexander to tell him what they had seen.

Darius's bold move had taken him behind Alexander, cutting off the Macedonians from their supplies and lines of communication from the Aegean. He was now facing the vulnerable rear of Alexander's army. Alexander was trapped. Without supplies, he could not risk plunging on eastwards or southwards into enemy territory. He had no option but to turn back northwards and take on the massive Persian force. While Darius had at least 60,000 men, Alexander only had some 26,000 infantry and 5,300 cavalry. And this time he was up against professional Persian soldiers, not conscripts levied locally like those he had defeated at Granicus.

Darius had decided to lead the army into battle himself. His Athenian general Charidemus was opposed to this, pointing out that Darius would be staking his throne on a single roll of the dice. In the heated discussion that followed Darius lost his temper and ordered Charidemus's instant execution. As he was dragged away, Charidemus cried out that Darius would pay for this injustice with his throne and his life. When his temper cooled, Darius regretted killing his best general and honoured Charidemus with special funeral rites.[37]

At Myriandus, Alexander drove a four-horse chariot into the sea as an offering to Poseidon to stave off Darius's Phoenician fleet,[38] then took his men on a two-day march of over 70 miles in torrential rain. Halting for the night on the heights above Darius's camp, Alexander gave his men a hot meal and a rousing speech. The following morning as the Macedonians descended, they saw Persian lines stretched out for three miles before them on the other bank of the river Pinarus in well-prepared defensive positions. Darius himself stood in the centre in his gold chariot, surrounded by Greek mercenaries with the Cardaces, a Persian phalanx of military cadets, occupying the wings.

Alexander had already set out his troops in their battle array when he discovered that Darius had posted a force on a spur behind the Macedonian right wing. Alexander despatched some light infantry, archers and horsemen to prevent the Persians attacking his rear. Then he sent his phalanx to ford across the river to attack Darius's Greek mercenaries and the Persian right wing. At the same time, he led his Companion Cavalry in a move to the right. The inexperienced Cardaces on Darius's left wing moved outwards to counter Alexander's attack, spreading out the Persian line. A gap opened and Alexander wheeled to the left to attack it. Once the line was broken, he turned on the Persian centre in an all-out attempt to kill Darius and finish off the Persian empire with a single blow. Charging towards the royal chariot, Alexander received a wound in the thigh, it was said, from Darius himself.[39] As Darius's royal guard was cut down around him there was a real danger that his horses might bolt, carrying the Great King into the Macedonian lines. Abandoning royal protocol, Darius himself took the reins to steady them.

The Battle of Issus 333BC by
Albrecht Altdorfer (1480-1538).
Alte Pinakothek, Munich

Alexander mosaic in Pompeii.
Museo Nazionale, Naples

At this point, the Persians were winning the battle. The Macedonian phalanx was having trouble crossing the river and Alexander's cavalry on the left wing were barely holding their own. But Darius was in danger of being killed or captured by Alexander's audacious assault on the Persian centre. There was nothing for it. Darius scrambled onto a lighter chariot and fled from the field. The Greek writers have made out that he was a coward. In fact, Darius was widely acclaimed for his bravery. But Darius knew that if he chose an honourable death on the battlefield, his empire would split into the rival factions that had divided it before his accession and the invader would overrun the divided empire. So he returned to his headquarters at Issus, leaving the field to Alexander. It is thought that between 5,000 and 10,000 of his men were slaughtered, turning the river red. But the Macedonians also suffered heavy losses, with 450 dead and 4,000 wounded, a casualty rate of 15 per cent. In the aftermath of the battle, Alexander founded a new city, where the 4,000 wounded from the battle could settle. This was one of several cities he called Alexandria, a name that lives on as Iskenderun in Turkey.

After the battle was won Alexander headed off after Darius, but Darius fled over the mountains on horseback, discarding his

royal insignia and mantle. Alexander picked these up, along with Darius's bow and shield, keeping them as battle trophies. At nightfall he gave up the chase and returned to Darius's base camp, where he bathed in Darius's great tub, changed into Darius's robes, stretched himself out on Darius's luxurious couch and ate off Darius's golden plate.

This, it would seem, is to be king, said Alexander.[40]

But Alexander's dinner was interrupted by wailing coming from a nearby tent. Alexander went to find out what the commotion was all about and found Darius's mother Sisygambis, his wife Statira, his six-year-old son, and his daughters Barsine (or Statira) and Drypetis in mourning. A royal eunuch had seen Darius's captured chariot and the insignia Alexander had picked up and concluded that he was dead.

Alexander explained their mistake and treated them kindly,

When Alexander went to visit Darius's womenfolk after the battle of Issus, he was accompanied by his lover Hephaestion. Both men wore plain Macedonian tunics, but Hephaestion was the taller and more handsome of the two. The queen mother, Sisygambis, assumed that he was Alexander and fell to her knees in front of him. When the mistake was pointed out to her, she was terribly embarrassed.

Never mind, Mother, said Alexander. *You didn't make a mistake. He is Alexander too.*

Then, without showing the least fear, Darius's six-year-old son put his arms around Alexander's neck and asked for a kiss. Alexander remarked to Hephaestion that it was a shame that his father did not display the same courage.[41]

even promising to provide dowries for the daughters and bring Darius's son up in a way befitting his royal status. This was not without self-interest. Alexander believed that if he ingratiated himself with the royal family he might be able to legitimise his claim to the Persian throne.

In the Near East it was the custom for a new king to take over the wives and harem of his predecessor. However, Plutarch says that Alexander 'sought no intimacy' with Darius's wife Statira, though she was 'accounted the most beautiful princess then living'.[42] There are good reasons to believe that this is not true. Statira was captured in November 333 and died either in childbirth or as a result of a miscarriage in September 331.[43] Darius cannot have been the father of that baby.

Soon after the battle of Issus, Darius sent Alexander a letter offering him all countries west of the Euphrates for the return of his family.

'If I were Alexander,' said Parmenio, 'I should accept this offer.'

So should I, said Alexander, *if I were Parmenio.*[44]

Instead Alexander rejected in it the most insulting terms, accusing Darius of several crimes he had not committed, including murdering Alexander's father Philip and killing Arses and thereby coming to the throne of Persia by illegitimate means.

Alexander and Hephaestion meet Darius's family

Your ancestors invaded Macedonia and the rest of Greece and did us harm although we had not done you any previous injury. I have been appointed commander-in-chief of the Greeks and it is with the aim of punishing the Persians that I have crossed into Asia, since you are the aggressors, he said.

He also accused Darius of turning the Spartans and other Greeks against him. *Your envoys corrupted my friends and sought to destroy the peace which I established among the Greeks,* Alexander claimed. And he boasted of defeating in battle *first your generals and satraps, and now you in person and your army, and by the grace of the gods I control the country.* If Darius wanted to write to him again, Alexander said, he should address him, not as an equal, but as *king of Asia* and *master of all your possessions. If not, I shall deal with you as a wrongdoer. If you wish to lay claim to the title of king, then stand your ground and fight for it; do not take to flight, as I shall pursue you wherever you may be.*[45]

It was partly thanks to Parmenio himself that Alexander no longer needed to make terms with Darius as Parmenio urged. After the battle of Issus, Parmenio had made a 220-mile dash across enemy territory to Damascus where he surprised the Persian garrison and captured almost 55 tons of gold and a great quantity of silver, coin and jewels. Parmenio needed 7,000 pack animals to return the booty to Alexander. On the long trudge back, winter closed in and the porters kept themselves warm by wrapping themselves in Darius's gold and purple robes. The gold and silver was later used to strike new coins, showing the head of Alexander's legendary ancestor Heracles with Alexander's features and on the reverse the supreme god Zeus seated on a throne.

'Alexander, esteeming it more kingly to govern himself than to conquer his enemies, sought no intimacy with any one of them, nor indeed with any other women before marriage, except Barsine, Memnon's widow, who was taken prisoner at Damascus. She had been instructed in the Greek learning, was of a gentle temper, and by her father, Artabazus, royally descended, with good qualities, added to the solicitations and encouragement of Parmenio, as Aristobulus tells us, made him the more willing to attach himself to so agreeable and illustrious a woman.'

PLUTARCH OF CHAERONEA[46]

At Damascus Parmenio also captured Darius's household staff which included 329 musically trained concubines, 306 cooks, 17 bartenders, 13 pastry chefs, 70 wine waiters and 40 scent makers, along with the wives and children of a number of Darius's commanders and relatives. Among them was Barsine, the widow of Memnon of Rhodes and, before that, his brother Mentor. She was some seven or eight years older than Alexander. The two had already met, when she, Memnon, her father Artabazus and her brother Pharnabazus had been exiled in Macedonia. Now their childhood friendship was renewed as a serious love affair and in 327 she gave birth to Alexander's first-born child, a son he named Heracles.

The Invasion of Egypt
332 to 331

After his victory at the battle of Issus, Alexander could have pursued Darius east and marched on Persepolis, the Persian capital. Destroying Persepolis would have paid the Persians back for Xerxes' attack on Athens in 480 and finished the war – at least as far as the Greeks were concerned. But Alexander's supply lines were still under threat from the Persian fleet under Pharnabazus, which controlled the Aegean Sea and menaced the Hellespont. So Alexander turned south to take the Phoenician towns of Aradus, Tripolis, Byblus, Beirut, Sidon and Tyre in modern-day Syria and Lebanon, intending to prevent Pharnabazus from using these ports to rest and resupply his ships.

There was another prize in his sights to the South – Egypt. Greece suffered regular food shortages. The Nile Valley was the breadbasket of the Near East and if Alexander could secure regular supplies of wheat from Egypt he could expect the lasting gratitude of the Greeks. Alexander also wanted to go to Egypt because his legendary ancestors Heracles and Perseus had done so.

Most of the Phoenician towns – Aradus, Tripolis, Byblus, Beirut and Sidon – surrendered as soon as Alexander approached and withdrew their fleets from the Persian force. But Tyre was put under siege. There was no strategic necessity to capture Tyre. Indeed the city had offered to surrender, but it had refused Alexander the right to sacrifice in the temple of Melkart – the Phoenician version of Alexander's ancestor Heracles – during the great festival in February on the grounds that only a native king could perform religious rites. No Persian king had made such a demand and the Tyrians insisted on remaining neutral until the war between Macedonia and Persia was over. However, when Alexander sent heralds to negotiate, they were killed and their bodies thrown over the battlements.[47]

The siege began in January 332 and it had an immediate advantage for Alexander. The Tyrians were forced to recall their ships from the Aegean. The other Phoenician towns that had surrendered had already done so. So, with the siege of Tyre, the Persian naval offensive in the Aegean came to an end and the threat to Alexander's supply lines lifted.

However, it was clear that the siege was going to be a long one. While the fortifications of Halicarnassus had been protected by a ditch only 50 feet wide, the citadel of Tyre was built on an island half-a-mile out to sea. The Macedonians began building a mole to reach the Tyrian walls. This was an extremely hazardous operation as the channel was over 20 feet deep and lashed by southwesterly winds. Above the strait the city's walls stood 150 feet high and they were so thick that the inhabitants believed they could resist even the strongest battering ram. The Tyrians also commanded the sea and harassed the construction of the mole which, at first, they thought was a joke. This only spurred Alexander on. Performing such an impossible task was a labour worthy of his ancestor Heracles (Hercules to the Romans). Indeed, Alexander told his men that, in a dream, he had seen Heracles standing on the walls, a clear sign that they were going to take the city.[48]

Alexander succeeded in building the mole with cedar bought from the Beqaa valley and rubble produced by demolishing the town of Old Tyre on the mainland. And with the other Phoenician cities now in his hands, Alexander could commandeer ships to protect the construction. Over the centuries, his mole has been covered with sand, forming an isthmus that remains a permanent feature of modern-day Sur in Lebanon. However, the mole

The siege of Tyre

was not used to take the city. Instead, he used the Phoenician ships to destroy the Tyrian fleet, while Macedonian ships carried siege engines up to the walls. According to the Roman writer Quintus Curtius Rufus Alexander himself led the attack, climbing the highest siege-tower. 'His courage was great, but the danger greater for, conspicuous in his royal insignia and flashing armour, he was the prime target of enemy missiles. He transfixed with his spear many of the defenders on the walls, and some he threw headlong after striking them in hand-to-hand combat with his sword or shield, for the tower from which he fought practically abutted the enemy walls.'

Soon the repeated battering of the rams had loosened the joints in the stones and the defensive walls had fallen down. Alexander's fleet had entered the port and Macedonian troops had made their way on to the towers the enemy had abandoned.

Some 6,000 Tyrian soldiers were killed fighting in the narrow streets, often making suicidal attacks, determined that their deaths should count for something. Others stood on the rooftops showering the Macedonians with stones. Alexander used public heralds to spread the word that no Tyrian under arms was to be spared. Civilians – mainly children – sought refuge in the temples. Alexander ordered his men to burn them down. Other Tyrians committed suicide or stood in the doorways of their homes, waiting to be cut down.

The Macedonian casualties were also heavy – around 500 killed, 4,000 wounded. In retribution Alexander had 2,000 Tyrian men of military age crucified on the beach. The other 30,000 survivors were sold into slavery. However, it is estimated that some 15,000 were saved by Sidonian sailors who recognised the Tyrians as fellow Phoenicians and smuggled them out of the city.[49]

Alexander went to the temple of Melkart to make his long-delayed sacrifice. He ripped the golden cord from the image of the god and renamed it, by decree, Apollo Philalexander (that is, Apollo who loves Alexander). Alexander then held triumphal processions and feasts. There were lavish funerals for the Macedonian dead, followed by games, naval reviews and torch races.[50]

Gaza was the next town to refuse to surrender. But Alexander was now master of the sea and his ships immediately brought siege engines to the city. However, its strong walls stood over 250 feet high on top of a hill and the siege engines were unable to destroy the fortifications. So Alexander's engineers burrowed under the walls instead. After four month's work, in October 332, the walls collapsed and Gaza fell. Its male population was killed to a man.

During the four months of digging, Darius had had time to form a new army. Alexander was furious when he heard the news. He had Batis, the Persian governor of Gaza, tied behind a chariot and dragged him around the city. According to Homer, Alexander's legendary ancestor Achilles had dishonoured the corpse of the Trojan warrior Hector in this way. It may have been customary in Macedonia to do so.

According to the Jewish historian Flavius Josephus, Alexander then made a pilgrimage to Jerusalem, though the story may simply be a Jewish legend.

'Batis was brought before the young king, who was elated with haughty satisfaction, although he generally admired courage even in an enemy. *You shall not have the death you wanted*, he said. *Instead, you can expect to suffer whatever torment can be devised against a prisoner.* Batis gave Alexander a look that was not just fearless, but downright defiant, and uttered not a word in reply to his threats. *Do you see his obstinate silence?* said Alexander. *Has he knelt to me? Has he uttered one word of entreaty? But I shall overcome his silence: at the very least I shall punctuate it with groans.* Thongs were passed through Batis's ankles while he still breathed, and he was tied to a chariot. Then Alexander's horses dragged him around the city while the king gloated at having followed the example of his ancestor Achilles in punishing his enemy.'

QUINTUS CURTIUS RUFUS[51]

Alexander portrayed as the Egyptian god Ammon

However, it is possible that the Jews supported Alexander during his campaign against Gaza and helped him in Egypt. The Persians had used Jews to garrison the southern border at Elephantine – or Abu, modern-day Jazirat Aswan, an island in the Nile opposite Aswan city. Alexander certainly used Jewish mercenaries to guard the city he was to build in Egypt, Alexandria.

Alexander headed on to Egypt. In late October 332, he reached Pelusium, modern-day Port Said, then started up the Nile towards the Egyptian capital Memphis. Mazaces, the Persian satrap of Egypt, and Amminapes, a Parthian Alexander had known in the Macedonian court in his youth, came out to meet him. Mazaces surrendered the country and presented Alexander with '800 talents and all the royal furniture'.[52] Amminapes had persuaded him that he had no choice. Darius had already taken troops from Mazaces' garrison for the battle of Issus. Darius's satrap also faced a restive population whose last rebellion against Persian rule had been put down just four years before. They greeted Alexander as a liberator.

The Persian kings had taken the place of the pharaohs of Egypt, so it was natural that Alexander should also assume that position. Entering Memphis he sacrificed to the Egyptian gods, especially Apis, the sacred bull whose cult was based in the city.[53] Then on 14 November 332 he was installed as pharaoh. With a double crown on his head and a crook and flail in his hand he was given the five royal titles of the Egyptian ruler. As both god and king, he became Horus the golden one, the protector of Egypt, king of Upper and Lower Egypt, the beloved of the creator god Amen, and the incarnation and son of Ra, the Sun god, and Orisis, god of the underworld.[54] The Egyptians accepted Alexander as their pharaoh when they heard the story of the snake that had visited his mother's bed (see chapter one). This was surely a sacred asp, the incarnation of Nectanebo II (360-343), the last native pharaoh. Alexander celebrated his elevation with a literary festival and more games.[55]

After he was crowned, Alexander sailed back up the Nile along the western or Canopic branch of the delta, past the old Greek trading port of Naucratis. Having destroyed Tyre, he wanted to transfer the hub of the eastern Mediterranean's maritime trade to Egypt. But Naucratis was 50 miles from the sea, so in January 331, Alexander decided to found a new seaport at the western mouth of the Nile. This was to be called Alexandria. The founding ceremony took place on 7 April, though Alexandria was actually built on the site of an older settlement. Archaeologists have discovered older walls and literary sources identify it as Rhacotis.

'After his conquest of Egypt, Alexander resolved to found and leave behind him a large and populous Greek city that would bear his name. On the advice of his architects he was about to measure out and enclose a certain site, when during the night, as he was sleeping, he saw a remarkable vision. He thought he could see a man with very white hair and of venerable appearance standing beside him and speaking these lines:

> There is an island washed by the open sea,
>
> Lying off the Nile mouth – seamen call it Pharos.[56]

He rose at once and went to Pharos, which at that time was still an island a little above the Canopic mouth of the Nile, but which has now been joined to the mainland by a causeway. When he saw that the site was eminently suitable, he . . . ordered the plan of the city to be drawn in conformity with the terrain.'

PLUTARCH OF CHAERONEA[57]

Plutarch tells the following story about the planning of Alexandria: 'Since there was no chalk available, they used barley-meal to describe a rounded area on the dark soil, to whose inner arc straight lines succeeded, starting from what might be called the skirts of the area and narrowing the breadth uniformly, so as to produce the figure of a mantle. The king was delighted with the plan, when suddenly a vast multitude of birds of every kind and size flew from the river and the lagoon on to the site like clouds; nothing was left of the barley-meal and even Alexander was much troubled by the omen. But his seers advised him there was nothing to fear; he therefore instructed his overseers to press on with the work.'

Alexandria would become a home for Alexander's wounded and his veterans, as well as emigrants from Greece. As a trading port it flourished and remains one of Alexander's few lasting achievements.

As preparations got underway, Alexander headed for the Siwah oasis some 250 miles across the desert to the west in Libya. This was home to the oracle of the ram god Ammon, whose cult had been introduced to Greece by the poet Pindar. Alexander would have known the shrine of Zeus Ammon in the Macedonian town of Aphytis, although there is no evidence that Alexander worshipped Ammon before he visited Siwah in February 331.

According to the Greek author Arrian of Nicomedia, Alexander visited the oracle because he wanted to imitate his legendary ancestors Heracles and Perseus, who had been there. Although Perseus never played an important role in Alexander's propaganda, since the 5th century, Perseus had been regarded as the ancestor of the Achaemenids, the Persian royal house. By identifying himself with Perseus, Alexander was proclaiming his right to rule in Persia.

The visit to Siwah also had propaganda value with the Egyptian populace. There were two temples in the oasis. One was built by the pharaoh Amasis (reigned 570-526); the other by Nectanebo II (reigned 360-343). Amasis was the last ruler of an independent Egypt before the Persian king Cambyses, son of Cyrus the Great, subjugated the country. Egyptians remembered Amasis' reign as a golden age. Nectanebo was king at the end of a period when Egypt had briefly reclaimed its independence between 380 and 343, but he had been defeated by the Persians and had fled. By visiting Siwah, Alexander was seen to be the 'returned Nectanebo', inaugurating a second golden age.

Alexander's meeting with the oracle took place in private. No one knows what questions were asked or what answers were given. However, after the visit, Alexander started to worship Ammon (the classical name for the Egyptian Amen, the king of the gods). He also insisted on being called 'son of Ammon' or 'son of Zeus', which amounted to the same thing.

During Alexander's stay in Egypt he sent his court historian Callisthenes of Olynthus upriver to Nubia – modern-day Sudan – on a diplomatic mission. Callisthenes took the opportunity to investigate the source of the Nile. It seems that he

'The journey along the coast as far as Paraetonium [modern Maras Matruh] was through deserted, though not waterless, country, for a distance of 175 miles according to Aristobulus. From there [Alexander] turned inland, where the oracle of Ammon was to be found. The road is deserted, sandy for the most part and without water. But Alexander had the benefit of heavy rains, and he ascribed this to the divinity. Another occurrence was attributed to divine intervention: whenever a south wind blows in that country, much of the road is covered with sand and the roadmarks disappear. One is in an ocean of sand, as it were, and it is impossible to tell one's direction, as there are no mountains or trees or solid hills to serve as signs and guide the travellers on their way, just as sailors go by the stars. Hence Alexander's army was advancing aimlessly and the guides could not tell the way. Ptolemy son of Lagus relates that two speaking snakes preceded the army and Alexander ordered the guides to follow them and trust in the divinity; the snakes then led the way to the oracle and back again. But Aristobulus says (and most writers agree with him) that two crows flew in front of the army and served as guides to Alexander. I can assert that there must have been some divine intervention to help Alexander . . .'

ARRIAN OF NICOMEDIA[58]

may also have discovered the reason for the river's annual flooding which made Egypt so fertile: Aristotle later wrote that the Nile floods were caused by the summer rains in Ethiopia, saying this had been discovered thanks to a Greek visitor who had witnessed them.

Alexander returned to Memphis via the Bahariya oasis, where a temple was built in his honour. Arriving back in Memphis in April, he received word that the Greek oracles at Didyma and Erythrae had confirmed that he was the son of Zeus. He also got news that the inhabitants of the Jewish city of Samaria, modern-day Sabastiyah on the West Bank, had revolted. It was time to return to Asia.

The Spoils of War
331

As Alexander marched up the coast towards Samaria in May 331 he heard that Andromachus, his military commander in Lowland Syria, had been burnt alive by the rebels there. When he arrived at Samaria, he destroyed the town and executed the rebel leaders. Samarians who fled and took refuge in the caves of Wadi Daliyeh were tracked down and killed, and the ruins of the city were given to the Jews of Jerusalem to resettle.

By late May, Alexander was back in Tyre, which had been resettled with veterans and loyal Phoenicians. He waited there for reinforcements – 15,000 men had been sent out from Macedonia that spring. By the end of July the reinforcements had arrived and a Macedonian army, consisting of 40,000 infantry, 7,000 cavalry and perhaps 2,000 supply wagons, headed east from Tyre. It crossed the Euphrates at Thapsacus. Up until this point, Alexander had been fighting in the Mediterranean world, which the Greeks knew well. But the country beyond the Euphrates was not well known, and the land beyond the Tigris was a mystery. And Darius had resumed his scorched earth policy and the skies were dimmed with a dark blanket of smoke.

In 401, Xenophon had marched 14,000 Greek mercenaries along the Euphrates to Babylon, then the richest city in the world. It may have been Alexander's intention to do the same. But, as his men were crossing the Euphrates, a Persian army, commanded by Mazaeus, satrap of Babylonia, approached from the southeast. Alexander could have attacked Mazaeus's army, but the battle would not have been decisive as Darius was not present and would have risked lives, weakening his force. Even if he were victorious the Persians would doubtless have employed a scorched-earth policy along the Euphrates, preventing further progress. To the east lay desert. So Alexander turned north, in the direction of Harran, where no Greek had gone before.

On the journey Alexander learnt that Darius had assembled an enormous army on the plains of Assyria and so turned to meet it. On 17 September 331 the Macedonians crossed the Tigris and almost immediately defeated a small squadron of Persian cavalry. But this was a diversion. Alexander had walked into another trap; he had been lured on to the battlefield of Darius's choosing.

The Persians had the military advantage, but the heavens seemed to be against them. The 'Astronomical Diary' written by the officials of the Esagila temple complex in Babylon, now in the British Museum, began to talk of fire falling from the sky and other ill omens. On the evening of 20 September, there was a lunar eclipse, almost immediately after the moon had risen in the east. The magi regarded the moon as a symbol of Persia. Worse, Saturn was close by – also a bad sign. 'Death and plague' were supposed to occur during the eclipse and it happened in the sixth month of the Babylonian calendar, a bad omen for the Great King of Persia. Together, all these signs pointed towards the eclipse of the eastern power. And there was a westerly wind, meaning that the end would come from the west. The signs could hardly be clearer. On top of that, Darius now heard that his wife had died, pregnant with another man's child. Again he tried to make a settlement with Alexander. Again Alexander refused.

A few days later, Alexander's advance guard located the Persians. They were camped near a village called Gaugamela or the 'camel's back'. His scouts counted thousands of campfires. Delighted that the decisive battle was almost in his grasp, Alexander ordered his army to make camp seven miles north of the Persian positions.

Darius was also pleased, bad omens notwithstanding. He had

Amphitheatre at Ephesus

been able to pick the terrain for battle and had established a supply base at nearby Arbela, modern-day Erbil. His general Mazaeus had forced Alexander to head for Assyria and his army had intentionally offered little resistance on the Tigris to lure the Macedonians onto the plain beyond, where a battlefield had been prepared. His men had levelled the ground for his 200 scythe-wheeled chariots to manoeuvre and spikes, stakes and snares had been placed on either side of the plain to prevent Alexander's cavalry from encircling the Persian army.

On the night of 29 September, Alexander led his men out in battle formation, intending to catch the Persians before they had made their dawn sacrifices, just as he had done at the river Granicus. But this time Darius's pickets saw the Macedonian army coming. The element of surprise was lost and Alexander called off the attack.

Alexander spent the 30th out on reconnaissance missions with a strong cavalry escort and it soon became clear to Darius that any attack would be postponed to 1 October. Parmenio suggested a night attack, but Alexander rejected this idea. Night attacks were always risky and Alexander felt that, to establish his authority over the

Persian empire, he must defeat Darius in the open, without any sort of trickery. However, he went out of his way to lead the Persians to believe that he was planning an attack that night. As a result Darius ordered his men to stand at arms all night. The following morning they were tired as well as demoralised by the astrological omens.[59]

Alexander himself slept soundly. After planning his attack late into the night, he fell into a deep sleep and was woken long after dawn by Parmenio who asked how he could sleep so soundly on the night before battle.

It is not remarkable at all, said Alexander. *When Darius was scorching the earth, razing villages, destroying foodstuffs, I was beside myself; but now what am I to fear when he is preparing to fight a pitched battle? By Heracles, he has done exactly what I wanted.*[60]

In fact, Alexander had done exactly what Darius wanted. Alexander's 7,250 horsemen now faced Darius's 34,000 front-line cavalry across a featureless plain, perfectly prepared for a cavalry battle. No amount of audacity, strategy or ill omen could get around the fact that the Macedonians were hopeless-ly outnumbered.[61]

Alexander's battle plan was very similar to the one he used in the battle of Issus. Parmenio was to hold the left wing, while Alexander and his Companion Cavalry would be on the right. Again Alexander would move to the right. The Persian left wing would have to do the same, or find itself outflanked. As the Persian line stretched, a gap would open. Alexander and the Companions would then turn, attack at that point and break through. The exact tim-ing of this charge was crucial. If the attack came too soon, before the weak point in the line had thinned sufficiently, the Persians would still be strong enough to fight him off; if it came too late, Alexander's troops would have spent too much of their strength attacking the Persian flanks, the Macedonian wings would cave in and the Companion Cavalry would be left fighting for its own exis-tence.[62] To increase the odds of success, Alexander kept 6,700 mercenaries in reserve behind his right flank, ready to punch home this crucial assault. This had the added advantage of making his army look even smaller and weaker than it was and encouraging the Persians to commit their full strength prematurely.

The danger, of course, was that, being so heavily outnumbered, the Macedonians would be outflanked and encircled. So as they advanced, their wings hung back in an angled line, like the edge of an arrow, making it more difficult for the enemy to get around their flanks. Alexander also kept a second line of infantry behind the main Macedonian battle array. These troops could be sent to the flanks if the Persians tried to encircle them.[63]

Before the battle, both commanders addressed their troops. Darius invoked Mithra, whose festival – the *Mithrakana* – had occurred just two nights before on the equinox. He emphasised that this was a holy war rather than a struggle for political power. Alexander also invoked the gods. He reminded his Greek troops that he was descended from Zeus who would strengthen and defend them. To his Macedonians, however, he merely said he was their king who would bring them victory.[64]

Once battle was joined, Alexander's strategy must have been obvious to Darius. He had seen it before at the battle of Issus. But he had not come up with an effective counter and depended on superior numbers to win the day.

Bessus, the satrap of Bactria, led the Persian cavalry against Alexander's right. More and more men were thrown in until Alexander's cavalry, numbering no more than 1,100 men, was holding ten times that number. Then Darius sent in his scythe-wheeled chariots. Although writers and film-makers have made much of the heads and limbs lopped off by the scythes attached to the wheels of these chariots, as an effective weapon they were already outdated. A line of lightly armed troops that Alexander had posted in front of the main line dealt with the Persian chariots easily, bringing down the horses with javelins or stabbing the drivers as they galloped passed.

Detail from the so-called Alexander sarcophagus depicting realistic Persians and heroised Macedonians

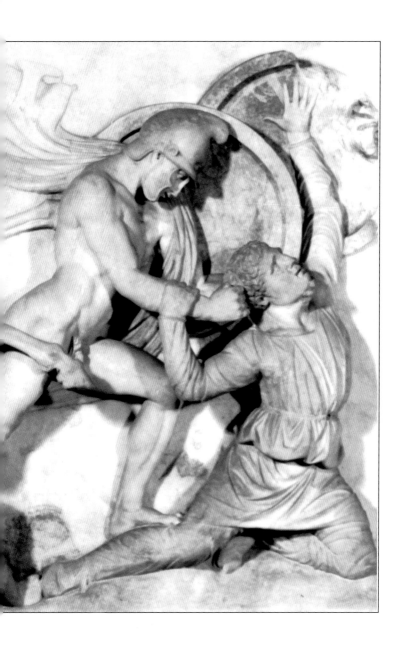

The Persian cavalry on the right wing, commanded by Mazaeus, outflanked Parmenio on the Macedonian left. But instead of turning and attacking the Macedonians from the rear, they galloped on to take the Macedonian camp seven miles behind the lines. Although they risked being surrounded, Parmenio and his men managed to hold their ground until Alexander stretched the line and spotted an opening. He charged with his Royal Squadron and the Companion Cavalry, followed by seven more cavalry squadrons, the Guards Brigade, some phalanx battalions and a welter of lightly armed troops. They smashed their way through the Persian line. Finding himself cut off from Darius's main formation Bessus sounded the retreat. Darius too seemed in danger of being cut off.

What happened next is unclear: the action was by now shrouded in dust kicked up by the battle. According to a contemporary Babylonian account[65] 'the troops of the king deserted him and . . . fled to the land of Guti' – that is, the valley of the Diyala, the shortest route to Ecbatana – the modern city of Hamadan in Iran, the ancient capital of Media and the summer residence of the Achaemenian kings. However, according to the Greek sources – Curtius Rufus, Plutarch of Chaeronea and Arrian of Nicomedia – Darius, cowardly as ever, fled from the battlefield. Only Diodorus of Sicily describes Darius as a great warrior.

Either way, Alexander emerged victorious, though he failed to kill or capture Darius. The Persian army was no more and Babylonia, the wealthiest satrapy of the empire, with its capital Babylon, the largest city in the world, lay at Alexander's feet. The Babylonians were not expected to put up any resistance as they had revolted against the Persian empire only five years before under the last independent Babylonian king Nidin-Bêl.

The Macedonians began collecting the spoils of war by looting the Persian camp. They plundered Arbela then marched quickly south towards Babylon. On the way, Alexander announced that he would spare the houses of the Babylonians so Mazaeus, who had returned to

Babylon, surrendered the city without a fight. He came out with his children to greet Alexander, who was delighted. Mazaeus was an eminent man who had distinguished himself in battle and his example was likely to encourage other satraps to surrender.

Babylon's royal treasurer, Bagophanes, organised an impressive reception. He carpeted the road with flowers and set up silver altars heaped with frankincense and other perfumes at intervals along it. He also brought out gifts – herds of cattle and horses, and lions and leopards, carried along in cages.

Next came the magi chanting a song in their native fashion. Behind them were the Chaldaean astronomers, then came the Babylonian musicians, whose job was to sing the praises of the Persian kings, equipped with their national instruments. The townspeople came out to greet Alexander, who was surrounded by an armed guard, and the Babylonian ceremonial cavalry brought up the rear. Despite this reception, Alexander formed up his men and advanced towards the city as if they were going into battle.

On 21 October 331, he entered Babylon through the famous Istar Gate, while crowds on the parapets showered roses down on him. Then the army marched down the Procession Street with the king at its head riding on the royal chariot.[66]

Alexander and his men were impressed by the beauty and antiquity of Babylon. It was the greatest city in what is now Iraq and had been the centre of the civilised world for three millennia. Founded by the legendary Queen Semiramis, it had at its core a huge citadel that straddled the Euphrates. This had been built by the Old Testament's Nebuchadnezzar two-and-a-half centuries before. Its outer wall was made of small baked bricks cemented together with bitumen. It was said to be 82 feet high and over 30 feet wide – wide enough for two chariots to pass each other safely on top of it. Although crumbling with age, the ramparts were still said to 'gleam like burnished bronze' in the autumn sunlight.[67]

Iskandar (Alexander the Great) lassoing Kintal, the Russian champion.
Persian illustration, c1540, British Library, London

The city was divided into ten quarters, each with its own gate. A religious capital, it had three huge temples to the great gods, 900 temples to the lesser gods and hundreds of neighbourhood shrines. The city was crossed by 24 great boulevards. There was enough green space between the buildings for the city to feed itself if besieged. And the whole town was surrounded by a network of canals.

One of the great wonders of Babylon was the stone bridge that connected the two parts of the city. On the north side of the Euphrates stood Nebuchadnezzar's palace. This had four great courtyards with their upper walls decorated with bands of enamelled brick. Their cedar-wood doors were inlaid with geometric patterns of gold, silver and ivory. The roof of the palace was supported by gilded cedar beams from Lebanon. The king's private residence boasted an audience hall and a plunge bath, while the bedroom over-

'Alexander's stop in Babylon was longer than anywhere else, and here he undermined military discipline more than in any other place. The moral corruption there is unparalleled; its ability to stimulate and arouse unbridled passions is incomparable. Parents and husbands permit their children and wives to have sex with strangers, as long as this infamy is paid for. All over the Persian empire kings and their courtiers are fond of parties, and the Babylonians are especially addicted to wine and the excesses that go along with drunkenness. Women attend dinner parties. At first they are decently dressed, then they remove their top-clothing and by degrees disgrace their respectability until (I beg my reader's pardon for saying it) they finally throw off their most intimate garments. This disgusting conduct is characteristic not only of courtesans but also of married women and young girls, who regard such vile prostitution as "being sociable".'

QUINTUS CURTIUS RUFUS[68]

looked the royal gardens on one side and the royal quay on the other. To the north, you could see the fabled Hanging Gardens with their pavilions and trees. The gardens were watered by cascades provided by the canals beyond and produced fruits, dates, grapes and pomegranates.

The Babylonians accepted Alexander as their new ruler and 'king of the world' as he now insisted on being called. His men were treated royally. They were billeted in luxurious houses and entertained by professional courtesans and enthusiastic amateurs. Although the practice of temple prostitution described by the Greek historian Herodotus the century before seems to have died out, it left a lascivious legacy and striptease was a popular after-dinner entertainment at drunken parties.

One of Alexander's first acts as 'king of the world' was to re-install Mazaeus as satrap of Babylonia. He was the first of a number of Persians to hold important offices under Alexander. It was a shrewd move. Alexander was fast running out of competent officers to administer his conquests. It also encouraged other satraps to surrender, on the understanding that they would be able to keep their posts. However, his own men saw this as the first sign that Alexander was being corrupted by the east.

One of the most important discoveries that Alexander's men made in Babylon was the Astronomical Diary of the Esagila temple complex of the Babylonian supreme god Marduk. For centuries, the officials there had systematically recorded celestial phenomena. One of the astronomers of Esagila, Kidinnu, was the first to give an accurate estimate of the length of the year, which he calculated to be 365 days, 5 hours, 44 minutes, 12.52 seconds, just 4 1/2 minutes away from the modern figure of 365 days, 5 hours 48 minutes, 45.17 seconds. The Astronomical diary was translated into Greek and Callisthenes of Olynthus sent it to his uncle Aristotle. The new knowledge was used immediately. The Greek astronomer Callippus of Cyzicus recalculated the length of the lunar month and devised a new calendar. This began at 28 June 330, eight months after the capture of Babylon.[69]

After five weeks of rest and recreation (much of it debauched) in Babylon, Alexander's men were on the march again. Newly reinforced, their next objectives were the four capitals of the Persian empire – Susa, Persepolis, Pasargadae and Ecbatana. During the march on Susa, modern-day Shush, Alexander reorganised his army. Until then, the Macedonian military units had been arranged according to the province the soldiers in the unit came from and were commanded by local men – a Thessalian always commanded the Thessalian cavalry and so on. From now on, officers would be selected on merit.

The Macedonians reached Susa in December 331. The commander of the garrison, the Persian Abulites, immediately surrendered and was appointed as satrap of the region, which was called Susiane by the Greeks, but better known as Elam and corresponds to modern-day Khuzistan in Iran. Leaving 1,000 veterans there, Alexander marched on towards Persepolis, the holy city of the Persian empire, the repository of its treasure and the burial place of the Achaemenid kings, who had ruled over Persia since 559.

Between Susa and Persepolis lay the Zagros mountains. Alexander faced a choice. He could try and force his way through a pass known as the Persian gates, a deep gorge across which the local satrap Ariobarzanes had built a defensive wall that was generally believed to be impregnable. Or he could skirt around the mountains to the south. But this would give the Persians time to evacuate Persepolis and its gold reserves.

Staircase at the palace of Persepolis: relief of tribute bearers bringing offerings to Darius the Great

Alexander hedged his bets. He divided his troops and sent Parmenio with the baggage train and the heavily armed troops on the southerly route around the mountains, while he himself led a column of lightly armed shock troops down the main road through the mountains to the Persian gates. Alexander reached the pass after a five-day march to find it heavily defended. Ariobarzanes and his men rolled boulders down from the sides of the steep gorge, accompanied by showers of arrows. The Macedonians suffered heavy casualties and Alexander was forced to withdraw – but not before he had taken some prisoners.

One of them, a shepherd, knew of a steep mountain track that bypassed the Persian gates and emerged behind the enemy. Alexander left 500 cavalrymen and two battalions of the phalanx under the command of Craterus at the entrance to the gorge. They were told to keep enough campfires for the whole army burning. Meanwhile Alexander and the rest of his men took a 12-mile detour along the mountain track. This was so gruelling that it

took them two nights, but they arrived behind Ariobarzanes' lines just before dawn on the third day. Two pickets were killed; then the trumpets were sounded. This was the signal to Craterus to launch another frontal attack, while Alexander and his men came swarming down the crags from the rear. Only Ariobarzanes and a handful of men escaped the onslaught. The rest were slaughtered where they stood.

Having broken through the Zagros mountains, Alexander headed for Persepolis. On the way, he met a band of Greek mercenaries who had earnt the displeasure of the former Persian emperor Artaxerxes III Ochus. Their ears and noses had been cut off, and they had been branded on the forehead. Some had also had their hands cut off, others their feet. Alexander offered to send them home, but they declined. In Greece, they said, they would be dispersed and become outcasts and objects of pity. They would rather stay where they were and form their own community. Alexander gave them seed corn, livestock, tools and cash – all they needed to start up as small farmers – and granted them tax-exempt status in perpetuity.[70]

Alexander entered Persepolis on 31 January 330. The governor surrendered the city and its treasures without a fight and, like Mazaeus, was reappointed.[71] But after an inflammatory speech in which he described Persepolis as 'the most hateful of the cities of Asia',[72] Alexander let his men sack the city – with the exception of Darius's palaces where the treasure was stored. They were allowed to kill any adult male they encountered and to rape and pillage as they pleased. Many of the inhabitants fled. Others committed suicide.

While his men were looting the private houses, Alexander visited the royal treasure-vaults, which contained 120,000 talents dating back two centuries to the time of Cyrus the Great. Another 8,000 talents of gold were taken from Darius's bedchamber. In all Alexander took bullion worth £2.3 billion at today's prices, which represented nearly 300

'Inside the chamber there was a golden coffin containing Cyrus's body, and a great divan with feet of hammered gold, spread with covers of some thick, brightly-coloured material, with a Babylonian rug on top. Tunics and a candys – or Median jacket – of Babylonian workmanship were laid out on the divan, and (Aristobulus says) Median trousers, various robes dyed in amethyst, purple and many other colours, necklaces, scimitars and inlaid earrings of gold and precious stones. A table stood by it, and in the middle of it lay the coffin which held Cyrus's body. Within the enclosure, by the times the annual national revenue of the Athenian empire in its 5th-century heyday. It needed no less than 5,000 camels along with every pack animal that could be commandeered in Babylon and Susa – 10,000 in all – to carry it.[73]

While Alexander was at Persepolis he visited the old capital of Pasargadae, 50 miles to the north. Again the Persian governor surrendered and handed over 6,000 talents from the treasury. Alexander also visited the tomb of Cyrus the Great there. New Persian kings were traditionally installed at a temple near to the tomb in a ceremony that involved consuming figs, turpentine and sour milk while wearing Cyrus's robe.[74] But Alexander could not don the mantle of Cyrus until Darius was dead.

Alexander stayed at Persepolis for more than four months. This made little military sense as it gave Darius the opportunity to raise another army. It seems that Alexander wanted to celebrate the New Year festival, held in Persepolis in April, as if he were the ruler of Persia. The Persian nobility normally went to Persepolis for the festivities. But that year only those who had already been given positions by Alexander turned up. So there were no celebrations and Alexander burnt the city down.

There are two versions of how this came about. Arrian said that Alexander burnt the city as retribution for the destruction of Athens by Xerxes in 480. His source was Ptolemy, a close friend

way which led up to the tomb, a small building had been constructed for the magi who guarded it, a duty which had been handed down from father to son ever since the time of Cyrus's son, Cambyses. They had a grant from the king of a sheep a day, with an allowance of meal and wine, and one horse a month to sacrifice to Cyrus. There was an inscription on the tomb in Persian, signifying:

O man, I am Cyrus son
of Cambyses,
who founded the empire
of Persia
and ruled over Asia.
Do not grudge me my
monument.'

ARRIAN OF NICOMEDIA[75]

of Alexander and an eyewitness. Plutarch, Quintus Curtius Rufus and Diodorus tell another story based on the account of the historian Cleitarchus, who wrote a quarter of a century after the event. He said that the Athenian courtesan Thais persuaded Alexander to burn the city down after a heavy drinking session.[76]

There is something to be said for both accounts. Archaeologists have shown that the temple of Xerxes was more severely damaged than other buildings. The rest of the city was not completely destroyed: there is evidence of human habitation after the fire. And preparation for the arson would have taken time – long enough for Alexander to sober up. The fire also made strategic sense. Alexander now had to pursue Darius across unknown country to the east and it would always be possible for the Persian king to double back and re-establish himself as ruler of Persia at Persepolis as long as the capital still existed.

On the other hand, it can be shown that the fire started in the treasury, before all the precious objects had been removed, indicating that it might have been started on a whim. Interestingly, Thais was the lover of Arrian's source Ptolemy – indeed, she was the mother of three of his children.

In May Alexander and his army set off for Ecbatana – modern-day Hamadan. This was the northern capital of the Achaemenid

Ptolemy I Soter (367-282) was a friend of Alexander from his youth. He fought in the battle of Issus, accompanied Alexander on his visit to the oracle of Ammon and was present during the burning of Persepolis. He was not one of Alexander's main commanders, but remained one of his most trusted friends and served as the taster of the royal food. After Alexander's death, he became satrap of Egypt, proclaiming himself king in 305. His dynasty ruled Egypt until the death of Cleopatra in 30BC. Ptolemy wrote a memoir on Alexander's campaigns, which has been lost but is known from Arrian's *Anabasis*.

empire, capital of the satrapy of Media and Darius's last stronghold. They arrived in June, but Darius had already moved on. He had wintered in Ecbatana in the hope of raising a new army, but had fled to the east before his new soldiers had turned up, only a few days before Alexander arrived.

By now Darius was losing support even among the royal family. Prince Bisthanes, the son of the former king Artaxerxes III Ochus, surrendered Ecbatana to the Macedonians and Alexander appointed a Persian named Atropates satrap of Media. At Ecbatana, Alexander quickly reassessed the situation. The burning of Persepolis and the palace of Xerxes had paid the Persians back for the destruction of Athens and essentially ended the Panhellenic crusade. The trouble in Greece was over and he no longer needed to hold Greek troops as hostages. He paid off the troops granted him by the League of Corinth, including the Thessalians who had been under the control of Parmenio. Cavalrymen were paid one talent – 6,000 drachmas – and infantrymen 1,000 drachmas. These were huge sums: one drachma was an ordinary soldier's daily wage. Alexander then offered anyone wanting to re-enlist as a mercenary three talents – 18,000 drachmas. The rest were given a cavalry escort back to the Mediterranean coast and shipped home. From now on, the war would not be waged for the League of Corinth or Greece, but in the name of Macedonia alone.

Alexander never cared much about money and was similarly generous to his Macedonian troops. By turning his army into a mercenary force, Alexander also sidelined Parmenio. The troops' first allegiance was now not to their commander, but to their royal paymaster.[77]

To the east, Darius travelled slowly because he was carrying the treasury of Ecbatana with him. He headed for Rhagae – modern-day Rayy near Tehran – the most important religious centre of Zoroastrianism, the Persian religion. It seems he want-

Stone relief from the palace in Persepolis

ed to sacrifice to the sacred fire there, but there was no time to stop and he headed on to the satrapy of Parthia to the east. His aim was to reach the distant eastern satrapy of Bactria, north of modern-day Afghanistan.

The satrap of Bactria was the most important man in the Achaemenid empire after the king. The post was traditionally occupied by a crown prince or, if the king had no sons, his brother. The present governor of Bactria was Darius's general Bessus, who was closely related to Darius and had claims on the throne himself. Bessus and Barsaentes, the satrap of Arachosia and Drangiana to the south, feared that if they remained loyal to Darius, the Macedonians would invade the eastern satrapies. So they arrested him, hoping that, if they handed him over, they would be able to keep their lands.

By now Alexander and his cavalry were in hot pursuit. After ten or twelve days, they arrived at Rhagae. Two days later, Alexander was in Parthia, where he heard that Darius had been arrested. However, he did not open negotiations with his captors. Alexander realised that, if he accepted Darius from Bessus, the price would be the eastern satrapies – half the empire (by area though not by wealth) he hoped to conquer. Worse, Alexander would then have to decide what to do with Darius. He was a threat as long as he remained alive, but the Persians might not take it too kindly if he murdered him.

So, in July 330, Alexander set off after Bessus and the retreating Persians. Against all advice he took a short cut across a waterless desert with his toughest and fittest men. After a 50-mile dash through the night they overtook the Persians at first light a little east of modern Damghan. When the Macedonian advanced guard rode up, Bessus panicked and had Darius murdered,[78] making his co-conspirators run him through with their javelins before leaving him to die. A Macedonian soldier named Polystratus, finding the dying king still chained in a bullock cart with his royal robes stained with blood and the javelins protruding from his chest, brought him some water in his helmet. Darius clasped his hand and thanked the heavens that he had not died alone and utterly abandoned.

Polystratus brought the news to Alexander, who seemed genuinely upset by his adversary's ignoble end. He covered Darius's body with his own cloak and had the corpse returned to Persepolis where Darius was given a state funeral.[79] In an attempt to legitimise his succession, he sent word to have the palace of Xerxes restored and set off in pursuit of the regicide Bessus, who now assumed the kingship as Artaxerxes IV.

With Darius now dead, the Macedonian troops thought the war was over. Alexander awoke one morning to hear wagons being loaded for the long trip home. His commanders warned him that if he tried to stop the

Four centuries later Arrian wrote a damning epitaph for Darius: 'In military matters he was the feeblest and most incompetent of men; in other spheres his conduct appears to have been moderate and decent – though the truth may well be that, as his accession to the throne coincided with the declaration of war by Macedonia and Greece, he had no opportunity to play the tyrant.'[80]

men leaving he would have a mutiny on his hands. They did not understand why he wanted to pursue the killers of Darius, who he himself had tried so hard to kill. But Alexander knew he must pursue and kill the regicides if he was to claim to be Darius's legitimate successor. He particularly needed to kill Bessus, who had a better claim than his to be the king. And to control the Persian empire, he must take Bactria, traditionally its most important satrapy because it controlled trade to the east. So he addressed the troops, telling them that Persia was only at peace because of their presence. If they returned home now, in a few months' time they would find Bessus at the head of a new Persian army crossing the Hellespont. Until he was dead, their job was unfinished.

We stand on the threshold of victory, he told his men. Bessus's capital was just four days march away. What was that compared to the 5,000 miles they had already travelled? This was a lie. The capital of Bactria, Bactra – modern Afghanistan's Balkh, near Mazar-e-Sharif – was 462 miles away. But his men, knowing no better, cheered and agreed to go on.[81]

Bessus was a considerable foe. Under his command were the mounted archers of Bactria and Soghdiana, satrapies that covered the area of modern Uzbekistan, Tajikistan and Afghanistan. Alexander's first move was to invade Hyrcania, the region to the south of the Caspian Sea. Hyrcania was not important in itself, but if it fell into Bessus's hands while the Macedonians were moving east, he would be able to cut off Alexander's lines of communication. During the Hyrcanian campaign in August 330, one of the mountain tribes, the Madians, captured Alexander's famous horse Bucephalus. Alexander let them know that, if they did not give him back, he would kill them all and lay their country waste. They realised that Alexander was in deadly earnest and returned Bucephalus, accompanied by 50 tribal elders bearing gifts. Alexander held them hostage against future good conduct[82] and appointed Amminapes, the Parthian who had helped in the surrender of Egypt, satrap of the region.

The campaign in Hyrcania convinced other Persians that Alexander was serious in his aim to punish Bessus for the murder of Darius and many of the dead king's followers came over to his side, including Darius's brother Oxathres. Artabazus, the father of Alexander's Persian mistress Barsine, became a key adviser. And Darius's favourite Bagoas – 'an exceptionally good-looking eunuch in the very flower of his youth'[83] – became Alexander's new lover.

With the influx of Persians, Alexander began to adopt Persian ways. He copied their style of dress, wearing a white robe and sash – though he drew the line at anything so barbaric as the

19th century view of Alexander in Persian robes

Persian habit of wearing trousers. He wore the blue and white Persian royal diadem, but not the upright tiara that went with it. Bessus, as Artaxerxes IV, had no such misgivings and wore the full regalia. But Alexander had a more important accoutrement of Persian kingship. He had Darius's retinue of 365 concubines – one for each night of the year – said to have been hand-picked from the most beautiful women of Asia. In fact, he employed them 'rather sparingly' because 'sleep and sexual intercourse, more than anything, reminded him that he was mortal'.[84] But it was important for his authority for Alexander to be seen to be sleeping with Darius's women.

Alexander's adoption of Persian ways and his appointment of Persians to important positions in his court rankled with the Macedonians, who did not see why those they had defeated in battle should be rewarded in this way. The Macedonians made little effort to understand the people they had defeated. Amminapes, Artabazus, Barsine and Bagoas all spoke Greek as well as Persian, which helped them secure their important positions at court. But only one of Alexander's Macedonian commanders bothered to learn Persian.

At the same time, though Persian allies such as Artabazus, Barsine, Amminapes and Bagoas tried to smooth over any cultural misunderstandings, Alexander's efforts to ingratiate himself with his new subjects seem to have been in vain. He had a Zoroastrian priest recite incantations and prayers at his court, and such was the interest in Persia that Alexander's former tutor Aristotle, back in Macedonia, published a book about the Zoroastrian priesthood, since lost, called *The Magians*. But Alexander became known to the Persians as the 'evil-destined and raging villain' and was called *Guzastag* – 'the Accursed' – a title that had until then only been used to describe Angra Mainyu, 'the hostile spirit', the personification of evil and eternal opponent of the Zoroastrians' 'wise lord' Ahura Mazda. It prob-

> A foreign prince will arise and seize the throne
> For five years he will exercise sovereignty
> The army of the Greeks will attack –
> The Greeks will bring about the defeat of Darius's army
> They will plunder and rob him
> But afterwards the king will refit
> His army and raise his weapons again.
> Enlil, Shamsh and Marduk
> Will go at the side of his army and
> He will bring about the overthrow of the Greek army
> . . . The people who had gone through misfortune
> Will enjoy well-being . . . the land will be happy . . .
>
> THE DYNASTIC PROPHECY,
> WRITTEN ON A CLAY TABLET
> FOUND IN BABYLON, NOW IN
> THE BRITISH MUSEUM[87]

ably did not help that the new coins Alexander had struck showing him as Heracles, wearing a lion's skin, made him resemble one of Angra Mainyu's helpers. While the Macedonians complained about Alexander's going native, Zoroastrian tradition claims that Alexander 'killed several high priests and judges and priests and the masters of the Magians and upholders of the religion'[85], 'quenched many sacred fires' and 'caused great devastation'. It is likely that several apocalyptic texts from the Zoroastrians' sacred book *The Avesta* were composed during the reign of Alexander.[86] Many of the magi fled to Drangiana. Others found safety in the mountains of northern Media, where they were protected by the Zoroastrian satrap Apropates. More generally, Persian discontent emerged in the widespread belief that Darius was not really dead and would return at the head of a victorious army to throw out the Macedonians.

Across the Hindu Kush
330 to 328

After Hyrcania had been pacified, Alexander marched east along the Silk Road – the traditional route from the Mediterranean to China via modern-day Afghanistan, which ran through the satrapy of Parthia and then Aria, a satrapy famous for its wine. The shortest route to Bactria was to follow the Silk Road on across the Kara Kum desert, via the oasis of Margiana. But this route would leave the Macedonians vulnerable to Bessus's mounted archers. Instead, at Susa – modern-day Tus near Mashhad in Iran – Alexander turned south, taking a longer, safer route through Drangiana, Arachosia and Gandara, then across the mountains of the Hindu Kush.

Satibarzanes, the satrap of Aria, surrendered as Alexander approached. Alexander reappointed him, even though he had been one of Darius's murderers. But when Alexander had moved on, Satibarzanes revolted and massacred the Macedonian garrison. Leaving his main force under the command of Craterus, Alexander turned back with a flying column to attack the Arian capital of Artacoana. Satibarzanes fled to Bactria with 2,000 cavalry, but left the rest of his troops camped in a forest. Alexander set fire to the trees and burnt them alive. He sold the inhabitants of Artacoana into slavery and founded a new seat of government called Alexandria-of-the-Areians, now known as Herat in Afghanistan. He appointed Artabazus's son Arsames as the new and more reliable satrap.

Again Alexander was giving a Persian high office rather than a Macedonian. Alexander tried to quell discontent among the Macedonian ranks with feasts and drinking parties. He also encouraged his men to marry the concubines they had picked up on their travels.

However, it seems that there was a plot to kill Alexander in October 330. At the centre of it was one of Alexander's soldiers, a young man named Dymnus. His homosexual lover's brother Cebalinus reported the plot to Philotas, the commander of the Companion Cavalry and son of Parmenio. Philotas dismissed the story as a lovers' tiff and did not tell Alexander. However, with the aid of a royal page, Cebalinus managed to hide himself in Alexander's bathroom and told his story to the king while he was bathing.[88]

Although there does not seem to have been much substance to the conspiracy, Alexander cunningly used it to rid himself of Parmenio. When Dymnus was arrested, he tried but failed to kill himself by falling on his sword. When the badly injured alleged assassin was carried to Alexander, he asked him: *What great wrong have I planned against you, Dymnus, that you should think Philotas more worthy to rule the Macedonians than myself?*[89] Dymnus died, leaving the question unanswered.

Alexander's inner council agreed that he would not be safe while Philotas and Parmenio remained alive. But Philotas was a distinguished commander, one of the most important men in the Macedonian army. Arresting him openly would be a dangerous step. So Alexander disarmed suspicion by inviting Philotas to dinner. Then in the dead of night Philotas and others implicated in the plot were quietly arrested. Meanwhile, guards had been stationed on the roads to Ecbatana to stop any message getting through to Parmenio, who had remained behind at Ecbatana.

Philotas was accused of high treason. Under Macedonian law, he had to be tried by the army. But the case against him was threadbare. It depended largely on tittle-tattle supplied by Philotas's mistress, whom Alexander had suborned. Philotas was allowed to speak in his own defence. When he appeared before the court, he was clad in rags and had his hands tied, and Alexander mocked him for speaking in Greek, rather than the Macedonian dialect. But Philotas then proceeded to tear the prosecution case to shreds.

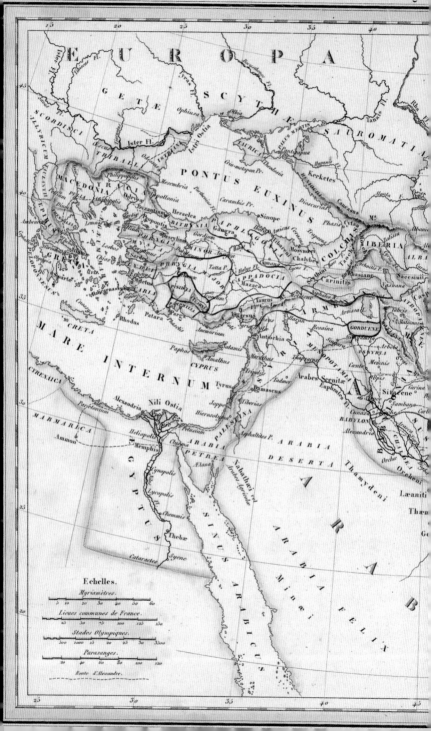

Empire D'ALEXANDRE.

C Y T H I A

MASSAGETÆ

CHORASMIE

Iaxartes fl.

Deserta

Bactius fl.

CHORASMII

Deserta

Cyropolis

Alexandriana

SACE

Paretacene

Gabæ

DAHÆ

Paphlagonia

Margiana vel

SOGDIANA

Nautaca

Mandrus

Comedi

Barganii

Deserta

Oxus

Marucæi

Varginia

Basistus

Alexandria

Ochus fl.

Alexandria

Characarta

Axiana

Alexandria

Oxus

Andaba banda Regio

Indus fl.

Issedon
Serica

Deserta

MARGIANA

Zariaspa vel Bactra

Aornus

Tochari

Gandari

Caspiri v.

IBISARI REG.

Merendropolis

Sapori

BACTRIANA

Drapsaca

Cauchasus M.

ISSICENI

Asmiræi

Zadracarta

vel Nysa

Taxari

Arigæa

Nysa

Alexandria

PARTHIA

NYSÆI

Tapuri

MARDI

Bactrus fl.

ISPIORI M REG.

Massaga

TAXILE REG.

Hecatompylos

Saphri

vel Paropamisus

Nicæa

Peucelaotis

Torontis fl.

Artacoana

Alexandria

PAROPAMISUS

Nysa

Aornus

PORI
REGNUM

Articene

ARIA

Phra

Alexandria

Sidus fl.

Abisari REG.

Hecatompylos

Ariaspæ

Arbari

OXYDRACÆ

Hydaspes fl.

Deserta

Tabiene

Lac. Aria

Prophthasia

Sacastene

ARACHOSIA

Alexandria

Ossadii

Alexandria

RETACE

Ecbatana Magorum

ZARINGE vel

DRANGA

Agriaspæ

Arachotus

Deserta

Ariacha

Ariaspæ seu Euergetæ

Alexandria

Arachotus fl.

Malaana

SOGDÆ

Alexandria

Carmania Deserta

Agriaspæ

Brems

M.

Parosi

Choarine

Cuni

MUSICANI R.

Carmania

Madomastia

Pura

Sindomana

Deserta

Pasagarda

Isthakhar

Salmente

GEDROSIA

Ora

Patala

Isthakhar

SICUS

Oaracta

Ichthyophagorum

Oræ

Malana

PATTALENA

Maces

Capella Pr.

phagi

Cophas

Padargus

Indi Ostia

Omana

Machorbe

Portus Occultus

Eirus M.

Sinus Canthi

Omanitæ

Pr. Carodamum

Pr. Didymi

E R Y T H R Æ U M   M A R E

INDIA

However, Philotas was an arrogant snob, unpopular with his men. They were reminded that he had once evicted them from their billets to make room for his possessions.[90] The trial was then adjourned.

That evening Alexander decided that a written confession from Philotas was required, preferably one that implicated Parmenio. Philotas was tortured by Alexander's closest confidants Hephaestion, Craterus and Coenus while he, according to Plutarch, directed proceedings from behind a curtain.[91] The following morning, Alexander had the confession he wanted, but continued the torture anyway. When Philotas was brought before the assembly to hear the sentence – death by stoning, the traditional punishment for treason – he could no longer walk.

A number of other prominent Macedonians of whom Alexander had become suspicious were killed along with Philotas. These included Alexander of Lyncestian, who had been denounced by Parmenio himself and had been held in close captivity for three years.[92] When he spoke up in his own defence, the guards, probably on Alexander's orders, ran him through with their spears.[93]

Next Alexander moved swiftly against Parmenio, who was now a real danger to him. Being stationed at Ecbatana, Parmenio controlled the road back to the Mediterranean. He had a large number of troops at his command, including reinforcements on their way to Alexander and, along with the quartermaster Harpalus, he also had control of the money Alexander had looted from Persepolis. Alexander sent messengers on racing camels that would reach Ecbatana in 11 days rather that the usual 30, to be sure they got there before the news of the death of Philotas reached his father. A courier gave a letter to Cleander, the commander of the reinforcements, ordering the commander to kill the old general. He also had a letter for Parmenio, written by his son under torture. As Parmenio was opening it, Cleander stabbed him in the ribs, then through the throat – then blows from other officers rained down on him. Although he never knew why he was killed, it would be wrong to

Alexander comforting a dying soldier. From the Shahnama, British Museum, London

feel very sorry for him. Parmenio himself had frequently employed extra-judicial murder as an instrument of policy.

Unlike Philotas, Parmenio had been popular with his men. They confronted Cleander, who showed them the letter contain-

ing Alexander's instruction to kill Parmenio. It clearly implicated Parmenio in the plot to kill Alexander. Parmenio's men
then demanded the general's body. At first Cleander refused,
only handing it over when they threatened mutiny. But first he
cut off Parmenio's head, which he sent to Alexander as proof he
was dead. The rest of the corpse was given a military funeral.
Although Alexander had finally rid himself of Parmenio, the
murder had serious political consequences. When Antipater
heard of it back in Macedonia, he said: 'If Parmenio plotted
against Alexander, who is to be trusted? And if he did not, what
is to be done?'[94]

Parmenio's men never forgave Alexander for his murder. To keep
abreast of what they were thinking, Alexander encouraged his soldiers to write home. He then opened their letters and read them.
Anyone expressing discontent or criticism was put into a discipli-
nary company that was used for particularly dangerous missions or
to garrison remote settlements on the eastern frontier.[95] However,
Alexander also listened to his men's grievances: he stopped appointing Persian satraps and began appointing Macedonians again. And
Alexander no longer trusted the command of the Companion
Cavalry to one man. He split the command between Cleitus and his
lover Hephaestion, who was given his first major post.

Alexander and the vanguard of his army continued their
march to the east, into what is now modern Afghanistan. In
December, the reinforcements joined them in the satrapy of
Arachosia. Its capital Kapisa – modern Kandahar – was renamed
Alexandria. Alexander then led his 40,000 men up the river
Tarnak along dangerous, snow-clad roads. On the way, he learnt
that Satibarzanes had returned to Aria and was inciting the people there to revolt. This was a serious threat to Alexander's rear
and he sent 6,000 men back to Aria, under Erigyius of Mytilene
and the trusted Persian officer Artabazus. They made short work
of Satibarzanes, with Erigyius killing him in single combat.

However, Aria remained troublesome and Alexander replaced its Persian satrap with a Macedonian. He also appointed a Macedonian satrap in Arachosia.

In March 329, Alexander's main force reached Gandara, also known as Parapamisadae, the area around modern Kabul. He established a garrison town there called Alexandria-in-the-Caucasus – modern Chârikâr – as a base for future operations. However the veteran Macedonian and Greek troops left there felt that their king had abandoned them in a remote colony as some kind of punishment, and there were several attempted insurrections.

Meanwhile Alexander pushed on across the snow-covered Hindu Kush on his way to Bactria. His strategy depended on speed. By spring, Bessus would have blocked the mountain passes. It was a gruelling journey. In places the lightly-clad Macedonians had to scale glaciers. They ran out of grain and consumed pressed sesame in lieu of olive oil, though it cost 240 drachmas per jar, along with honey and wine costing respectively 390 and 300 drachmas. Eventually they had to eat their pack animals. Alexander lost more than 2,000 men on the way, leaving him an army of 32,000. At the end of March, the Macedonians surprised the primitive mountain tribes near the Khawak pass. Two weeks later, they took Drapsaca – modern-day Konduz – in Bactria.

It is said that, during their march across the Hindu Kush, the Macedonians saw the cave of Prometheus. He was the demigod who stole fire from the gods and gave it to mankind. As punishment Zeus had him chained to a mountain for eternity and sent an eagle every night to devour his liver, which then renewed itself every day.

Bessus's army of 8,000 Bactrians thought that their harsh climate would discourage the Macedonians and they would head on into India instead. But once they realised that there was no escaping Alexander they abandoned Bessus and slipped off back to their villages. With only a handful of supporters, Bessus fled north across the river Oxus, now called the Amu Darya, into the satrapy of Soghdiana, burning his boats behind him. There he began recruiting the local Soghdians.[96]

A few days later, Alexander captured Bactra, the capital of Bactria, and appointed Artabazus satrap. He left his baggage there and proceeded with a lightly armed force. On the march onwards to the river Oxus, Alexander's troops entered a huge pebble desert area. Only weeks before the Macedonians had been suffering from frostbite. Now they suffered heatstroke. It was too hot to travel in the day and they were forced to march by night. For 50 miles no trace of water was to be found.

Quintus Curtius Rufus described their plight: 'The heat of the summer sun scorches the sands and, when these start to heat up, everything on them is baked as if by perpetual fire. Then a misty vapour thrown up by the burning heat of the earth obscures the daylight, giving the plains the appearance of one vast, deep ocean. Travel by night seemed bearable because dew and the early morning freshness would bring relief to their bodies; but with the dawn comes the heat, draining with its aridity all natural moisture and deeply burning the mouth and the stomach.

'So it was their resolution that failed first, and then their bodies. They were unwilling to stop and unwilling to go on. A few had followed the advice of people who knew the country and stored up some water. This slaked their thirst for a short time, but then the increasing heat rekindled their craving for water. Consequently, all the wine and oil in anyone's possession was consumed, too, and such was the pleasure they gained from drinking it that they had no fear of thirst in the future. Subsequently, the liquid they had greedily drained put such a weight on their stomachs that they could neither hold up their weapons nor continue their journey, and the men who had been without water now seemed to be more fortunate than they themselves, since they were forced to spew up the water they had immoderately consumed. . . .

'Finally, around early evening, Alexander reached the river Oxus, but most of the troops had been unable to keep pace with him. He had beacons lit on a mountain-peak so that men having difficulty keeping up could see they were not far from camp. Those at the front of the column, quickly revived by something to eat and drink, were ordered by Alexander to fill skins, or any vessels that could serve for carrying water, and to bring relief to their comrades. But some men gulped the water down too greedily and died from blockage of the windpipe – and the number of these exceeded the numbers Alexander had lost in any battle. As for the king, he stood at the point where the troops were arriving, still wearing his cuirass and without having taken any food or drink, and he did not leave to take refreshment until the entire column had passed him.'[97]

'At this point [Alexander] was met by two of the men who had gone ahead to select a campsite. They were carrying skins of water to bring relief to their sons who, they knew, were suffering from severe thirst in Alexander's column. On meeting the king one of them opened a skin, filled a cup he was carrying, and offered it to him. Alexander took it. Then he asked for whom they were carrying the water and learned it was for their sons. He returned the cup, as full as when it was offered to him, saying: *I cannot bear to drink alone and it is not possible for me to share so little with everybody. Go quickly and give your sons what you have brought on their account.*'

QUINTUS CURTIUS RUFUS

The Oxus was nearly three-quarters of a mile wide and Bessus had burnt all the boats in the region. Alexander's engineers tried to sink piles in the sandy bottom but they were carried away by the fast-flowing waters. Besides, there was not enough timber in the surrounding countryside to build a bridge. So Alexander got his men to stuff their leather tent covers with hay and stitch them up to make floats, with which they could swim across the river. Five days later, the Macedonian army was on the other bank of the Oxus in Soghdiana, in what is now Turkmenistan.

Bessus had assumed that Alexander would be halted by the Oxus but his judgement had again proved faulty. Now his men turned against him. The courtiers Spitamenes and Datames arrested Bessus and offered to hand him over to the Macedonians. Alexander sent Ptolemy to collect Bessus, giving him detailed instructions on how he should be delivered as a warning to any other Persian noble who turned against him. He was to be left with with a slave's wooden collar around his neck and bound naked to a post erected at the roadside where Alexander and his troops would march by.

When Alexander passed the post, he stopped the column. Then he stepped down from his royal chariot and asked Bessus why he had killed Darius *his king, kinsman and benefactor*. Bessus replied that it had not been his decision alone and it had been done 'to win Alexander's favour and so save their lives'. But Alexander was anxious to establish himself as Darius's legitimate successor, rather than a foreign invader who needed appeasing in this fashion. He had Bessus flogged. Bessus then stood trial for the murder of Darius and had his ears and nose cut off. The Greeks and Macedonians thought this was barbaric, but it was the traditional Persian punishment for a regicide. After the mutilation, Alexander handed Bessus over to Darius's brother Oxathres, who crucified him in Ecbatana in front of an invited audience of leading Persians and Medes. Alexander also ordered that vultures be kept away from his corpse. Zoroastrians believed that the dead must be devoured by birds. This was the Persian equivalent of denying Bessus a proper burial.

Alexander was now the unchallenged king of Persia, but his men continued to march northwards to establish the borders of his empire. There were some minor skirmishes, but by and large the fighting was over. They soon reached Nautaca – modern Shakhrisabz, a town famous throughout the Persian empire – and Maracanda – modern Samarkand and the capital of Soghdiana.

The army marched on to the river then known locally as Jaxartes – now called the Syr Darya. Alexander believed that this river was the Araxes, which his teacher Aristotle said had its sources in the Hindu Kush. One of its branches became the Tanais – now known as the Don – which was traditionally seen as the border between Asia and Europe. Alexander could now claim that he had reached the end of Asia. To celebrate, at the beginning of July 329 he founded a new city called Alexandria-the-Furthest, also known as Eschate, modern-day Khodzent in Tajikistan. This was to be a garrison town to protect the northern border against the Sacae, the nomadic tribes that inhabited the area beyond. It superseded an older city called Cyropolis, 'the town of Cyrus'.

It was five years since the battle of Granicus and Alexander's triumph seemed complete. Indeed his court historian Callisthenes of Olynthus ended his *Deeds of Alexander* with the founding of Alexandria-the-Furthest. But at this moment the Soghdians under Spitamenes revolted. The Sacae, along with the nomadic Massagetes and Dahae, joined their rebellion. These tribesmen were accomplished mounted archers and masters of the dusty steppe country there, which left the footsoldiers of the Macedonian phalanx vulnerable. Alexander responded by bolstering his cavalry with native Iranian horsemen.

Alexander had only 30,000 men north of the Hindu Kush to put down the revolt. With them, he captured seven Soghdian forts. Local towns were given the treatment meted out to Tyre. The men were killed and the women and children sold into slavery. At Cyropolis, 8,000 were killed in the fighting and 7,000 survivors were executed afterwards *en masse*. As a result subsequent resistance was ferocious. Alexander was wounded several times. An arrow hit him in the leg and in hand-to-hand fighting he was struck in the neck by a large stone. His vocal chords were damaged and his vision impaired. It was feared for a time he might go blind. And crossing the Jaxartes he drank some infected water, adding gastro-enteritis to his troubles.[98]

While Alexander was dealing with the seven forts, Spitamenes' besieged the Macedonian garrison at Maracanda. Alexander sent a relief column under Pharnuches, but it was ambushed and cut down almost to a man. Alexander threatened the handful of survivors with death if they told anyone what had happened. In just three days, he covered the 160 miles to Maracanda with a column of cavalry and lightly armed troops. He relieved the city but Spitamenes and his men melted away into the desert. Alexander soon gave up the pursuit and turned south again, laying waste the land to prevent Spitamenes returning to attack Maracanda again that winter. He also made a detour to the place where Pharnuches' column had been massacred to bury the dead.

All these actions cost lives and, by the end of 329, Alexander's army was so small that he was unable to continue the war. He wintered at Bactra, waiting for reinforcements to arrive from the west. These were the Greek mercenaries Antipater had used to crush a revolt in Greece in 330.

Alexander spent the winter drinking heavily. During a drinking party, sycophantic courtiers sought to belittle Alexander's father Philip and lauded Alexander as the son of Zeus Ammon. Alexander alone was responsible for the Macedonian victories, they said, and they made jokes about Pharnuches and the other commanders who had been killed by Spitamenes. Cleitus, who had served under Philip as a cavalry commander, took exception. The Macedonian army as a whole had contributed to Alexander's victories and he had known Pharnuches and the other men who had been killed by Spitamenes. A little drunk himself, he started to praise Philip and accused Alexander – who was now comparing himself to Heracles – of blasphemy. It was disgraceful of him to denigrate Philip and other Macedonians in front of his Persian courtiers, he said, and he reproached Alexander for the murder of Attalus. In rage Alexander grabbed the first thing that came to hand – an apple – and threw it at Cleitus,[99] then began looking around for his sword, which a bodyguard had sensibly removed. Perdiccas and other Companions intervened and held Alexander down, while Ptolemy and others tried to drag Cleitus out of the room. But Alexander broke free, grabbed a spear from one of his guards and ran Cleitus through, killing him on the spot.

When he saw what he had done, Alexander was overcome with grief. He pulled the spear from Cleitus's body and tried to impale himself. Restrained, he locked himself in his private quarters and refused to eat or drink. Soon his followers were frantic. If he succeeded in starving himself to death, they would be left leaderless in a hostile country thousands of miles from home.

Cleitus 'the Black' (c375-328) was the son of the Macedonian noble Dropides, who seems to have helped Philip become king in 359. His sister was Alexander's wet-nurse. Cleitus became an officer of the Companion Cavalry. He saved Alexander's life by running through the Persian commander Spithridates who had already sliced clean through Alexander's helmet with a battle-axe. Cleitus became one of Alexander's most trusted officers and after the murder of Philotas took over command of the Companion Cavalry jointly with Hephaestion and was named future satrap of Bactria and Soghdiana – a position usually occupied in the Persian empire by the crown prince. He did not live to take up the post.

For three days, Alexander contemplated suicide and, through lack of food and water, came close to death. Callisthenes tried to talk him round without success.[100] However, the philosopher Anaxarchus of Abdera convinced him that, as king, he was next to god and stood above human law. Alexander may also have been comforted by thoughts of his ancestor Heracles who, according to myth, had killed his wife and children in a fit of madness and undertook his Twelve Labours in expiation. So it was decreed that Cleitus had been justly put to death and Alexander lived on, even more convinced of his divine status.[101]

A Persian Wedding
328 to 327

When reinforcements arrived in the spring of 328, Alexander campaigned along the Upper Oxus and then returned to Bactra and divided his army. Two-thirds of the phalanx were left to defend Bactria. A second force of infantrymen under Hephaestion was to march north into Soghdiana and build six garrison towns. Artabazus and Coenus were to take a mixed cavalry into the extreme north of Soghdiana to take on the Sacae and Bactrian horsemen. Meanwhile Craterus was to go to the west to take the key oasis town at Margiana between Bactria and Aria in the Kara Kum desert to prevent it falling into Spitamenes' hands. Alexander, Ptolemy and Perdiccas were to attack the Soghdian mountain settlements in the Hissar range.

Although Spitamenes kept up a guerrilla war that brought the fighting dangerously close to the walls of Bactra, gradually the tribes of central Asia began to send ambassadors to make peace treaties with Alexander. When the Massagetes heard that Alexander himself was coming after them, they lost no time in executing Spitamenes. Curtius says that Spitamenes' wife, tired of life on the run, carried out the execution herself.[102] Spitamenes' head was sent to Alexander as a peace offering. When the neighbouring Dahae tribe heard of this, they handed over Spitamenes' second in command and the rebellion was over.

However, there were still mopping-up operations to be done. The Soghdians had retreated to huge rock-fortresses. Throughout the winter, Alexander continued his campaign. His army marched on through thunderstorms and torrential rain. Temperatures plummeted and some 2,000 men froze to death or died of pneumonia. Alexander rallied his troops and got them to cut down trees and light fires. One Macedonian who had been lost in the forest stumbled into camp barely able to stand. Alexander sat him in his own chair by the fireside to warm him. When the man realised whose seat he was sitting in he leapt to his feet. *Now do you see how much better a time you have of it under a king than the Persians do?* Alexander asked the soldier. *With them, to have sat in the king's seat would have been a capital offence – but in your case it proved a life-saver.*[103]

News had come in that a large number of the tribesmen had taken refuge on the Rock of Soghdiana. Among them was local nobleman Oxyartes the Bactrian, who had refused to submit to Alexander. He had chosen this refuge for his family in the belief that the Rock was impregnable. This was the last stronghold in Soghdiana. If it fell, resistance would be over.

At the start of spring, Alexander began to move on the Rock. When he reached it he found that it rose sheer on each side. Its occupants were provisioned for a long siege, and the deep snow that remained on its summit made the ascent difficult for the Macedonians while ensuring the defenders had an unlimited supply of water.

Alexander offered to allow the defenders to return to their homes unmolested if they surrendered the stronghold. They laughed and told Alexander to go and find soldiers with wings as no one else stood a chance of capturing the Rock. This only made Alexander all the more determined. He offered 12 talents (nearly 200 years' pay for an ordinary soldier) to the first man to scale the rock. The second would get 11, the third ten and so on to the 12th, who would 'receive 300 gold darics'.

In Alexander's army there were some 300 men who had experience in rock-climbing from previous sieges. They assembled and attached strong flaxen lines to small iron tent pegs, which they would drive into the snow, where it was frozen solid, or into any bit of bare earth. The party set off under cover of darkness. They headed for the steepest part of the rock-face, which was the least likely to be guarded. Driving their pegs into cracks in the rock or patches of ice, they hauled themselves up. About 30 fell during the ascent and lost their lives and their bodies were never recovered. But the rest reached the top as dawn was breaking.

They signalled to the troops below by waving pieces of linen, and Alexander sent a crier to shout the news to the enemy's advanced posts that men with wings had been found and they had already taken the summit. To reinforce the point, Alexander pointed to his men standing on top of the rock. Their presence took the defenders so much by surprise that they surrendered, though if they had put up a fight they could easily have finished off such a small force.

Among the prisoners were the wife and daughters of Oxyartes. One of his daughters was named Roxane. She was of marriageable age and men who took part in the campaign said that she was the loveliest woman they had seen in Asia, with the exception of Darius's wife. According to Arrian

Alexander marrying Roxane, daughter of Oxyartes

Alexander 'fell in love with her at sight; but, captive though she was, he refused, for all his passion, to force her to his will, and condescended to marry her'.[104] Lovely she may have been, but it is noteworthy she did not become pregnant until after the death of Hephaestion.

Alexander may have married Roxane purely for political reasons to help in the pacification of Bactria and Soghdiana. His new father-in-law Oxyartes, the most powerful of the Bactrian warlords, helped to persuade other leaders that further resistance was useless. In one case, Oxyartes convinced the commander of a rock fortress 4,000 feet high and seven miles in circumference to surrender, after Alexander had expended vast effort building a bridge across the ravine that led to the stronghold. Under the peace deal, Alexander left the commander in position in exchange for two months' rations for his entire army. This amounted to just one tenth of the rock's reserves, indicating that the fort could easily have held out.[106]

Had Alexander wanted a Persian wife he could have married Barsine, the mother of his son Heracles. But she had spent much of her early life in Macedonia and marrying her would not have been so politically useful to Alexander. However, marrying Roxane alienated Barsine's father Artabazus, who had played an important role in winning over the Persian elite.

Alexander defeated the warlords of Bactria and Soghdiana one by one, reduced the populace to serfdom and concluded treaties with the neighbouring nomadic tribes. Even so he had to leave an enormous garrison of over 11,000 men to hold Bactria and Soghdiana. With his army now dangerously short of men, Alexander ordered 30,000 young Iranians to be formed into a new phalanx called the 'Successors'. They were taught Greek and given Macedonian-style military training. He also added more local cavalry units to his Macedonian army and pressed the mounted archers of the Dahae into service. Not only did this give

Alexander much-needed manpower, when he marched on into India they served as hostages, as the Greek troops had before, quelling any temptation to rebel in Persia. However, his Macedonian veterans were unhappy. Not only had Alexander married one of the enemy, he was now filling his army with the men they had just defeated.[107]

Alexander managed to alienate his Macedonian and Greek followers even more with the introduction of *proskynesis*, the Persian custom of greeting a superior with bows, blown kisses and obeisance. When Alexander ordered his courtiers to prostrate themselves in front of him, the Greeks among them refused, saying that it might be appropriate for an Asian to express his loyalty that way, but not for a European. But Alexander realised that if the Macedonians and Greeks did not greet their king in this fashion the Persians might wonder whether he was really a king. So the introduction of *proskynesis* was a political necessity. Early writers connected the introduction of *proskynesis* with Alexander's growing belief in his own divinity, though he did not claim to be a god until 324 or 323.

Alexander first tried to introduce the custom during a drinking party in Bactra. The Persian philosopher Anaxarchus brought up the topic, saying that Alexander had much better claims to be regarded as a god than Dionysus and Heracles and the Macedonians should honour him accordingly. As they would treat him as a god once he was dead, when he would derive no benefit from it, wouldn't it be more sensible to honour him that way during his lifetime?

'When the Persians meet one another in the roads, you can see whether those who meet are of equal rank. For instead of greeting by words, they kiss each other on the mouth; but if one of them is inferior to the other, they kiss one another on the cheeks, and if one is of much less noble rank than the other, he falls down before him and worships him.'

HERODOTUS OF HALICARNASSUS[108]

Those who were privy to Alexander's plan praised Anaxarchus's words and said they wanted to begin doing obeisance to Alexander. But most of the Macedonians were displeased and kept quiet. Then Callisthenes, a Greek, spoke up.

'Anaxarchus,' he said. 'I declare that there is no honour fitting to man that Alexander does not deserve. But a distinction has been drawn by men between honours fit for mortals and honours fit for gods.' Alexander, for example, would not tolerate a private individual laying claim to royal honours on the strength of a show of hands. Surely the gods would be equally justified in showing their displeasure to those who assumed divine honours or allowed others to do it for them?

Callisthenes reminded Anaxarchus that it was not a Persian like Cambyses or Xerxes he was advising, but the son of Philip, descended from Heracles and Aeacus, whose forefathers came from Argos to Macedonia. They had ruled the Macedonians by law and not by force. Not even Heracles had been honoured as a god by the Greeks in his lifetime.

It might be necessary to adopt foreign ways in a foreign land, but, Callisthenes begged, Alexander should not forget Greece. His expedition had been launched in the name of Greece, to add Asia to Greece not the other way around. When he returned to Greece would he make the Greeks there – 'the freest of men' – prostrate themselves? Or would he make an exception for the Greeks but inflict this indignity on the Macedonians?

Although these words greatly irritated Alexander, the Macedonians were pleased to hear them and Alexander agreed to forget about the introduction of *proskynesis* for the time being. However, Persians in court continued to perform obeisance and when Leonnatus, one of the Companions, mocked the Persian's submissiveness, Alexander grew angry and decided to introduce *proskynesis* by stealth.

At a drinking party, Alexander passed round a golden cup,

handing it first to those who agreed to obeisance. One by one the men drank from it, offered obeisance and then received a kiss from Alexander. When it came to Callisthenes' turn, he drank from the cup and went to kiss Alexander – without offering obeisance. Alexander refused him a kiss.

'Well then,' said Callisthenes, 'I shall go away one kiss the poorer.'[109]

Callisthenes would soon pay for his levity. During a hunt, the Persian king was supposed to be the first to strike at the quarry. However, on one occasion one of Alexander's pages, fearing for the king's life, speared a charging boar, killing it. Alexander had the boy whipped. With the other pages, the boy plotted to murder the king in his bed. But that night Alexander got drunk and did not return to his tent. The plot was uncovered and the five pages were executed by stoning. It transpired that the boy who had been flogged had complained to Callisthenes, who told him to 'remember that he was a man now'. This was interpreted as incitement to murder and Callisthenes was either hanged immediately or confined to a prison cage that was dragged along behind the army until he died.[110] Once Callisthenes was out of the way *proskynesis* was introduced successfully.

By the closing months of 327, Alexander the Great had secured
the northern frontier of his Persian empire and was ready to move
on into India. There was no real need to do this. Alexander's
excuse was that he had to protect the eastern frontier of his empire
from attack through the Khyber Pass. He told Pharasmenes,
prince of Chorasmia, later Khwarezm in Afghanistan, who wanted him to fight the peoples of the northern steppes, that once he
had conquered India 'he would have Asia entirely in his hands'.
Cyrus the Great had been unable to hold onto his satraps in India
and even the semi-legendary Queen Semiramis had failed to
invade the subcontinent successfully. Alexander went on to say to
Pharasmenes that he planned a full-scale naval and military expedition to the Black Sea, giving the first indication of his plan for
world-conquest.[111]

Alexander's mythological kinsmen Dionysus and Heracles had
visited India. Dionysus, the Greek god of wine and ecstasy, was
said to have introduced the vine there, while Heracles begat a long
line of Indian kings.[112] Alexander wanted to outshine them both
and believed that the people of India would accept him as a god.[113]

India was a place that the Greeks already knew from literature.
Herodotus of Halicarnassus had written about it, but included
fabulous stories about ants the size of foxes that dug for gold.
Herodotus also wrote that Indians had black semen. Aristotle dis-
agreed, arguing that their semen was white because their teeth
were white. Ktesias, a Greek doctor who served in the Persian
court in the fifth century BC, wrote of men with dogs' heads and

tails, eight-fingered archers whose ears were big enough to shade them from the sun, men who had no heads but had eyes in their shoulders, pygmies with penises that hung down to their ankles and children who only acquired an anus at puberty.[114]

Alexander got a more realistic view of what lay beyond the Khyber from an Indian prince named Sasigupta – or Sisicottus – who had deserted from Bessus and joined the Macedonian's retinue. Alexander also sent envoys to Ambhi – also known as Omphis – the rajah of Taxila – or Takshaçila, modern Rawalpindi – who was inviting foreign help in his war against Porus, the powerful ruler of Paurava, the region beyond the Jhelum river – then known as the Hydaspes – in the Punjab.

At the end of 327, Alexander divided his army in two. The main force under Perdiccas and Hephaestion travelled through the Khyber Pass to the river Indus, where they built a bridge. On their way, they occupied a town called Peucelaotis – the Indian Puskalâvatî, modern Charsadda, north of Peshawar – after a month-long siege.

Alexander himself, with Craterus as his second in command, took a smaller force through the foothills of the Himalayas to the north to take the strongholds there and protect the flank of his main army. However, the Himalayan tribesmen were ferocious fighters and Alexander was injured in the shoulder with an arrow in the fighting there. He turned to tactics that were little short of genocide. Defenders were routinely massacred. At Massaga, the capital of the Himalayan tribesmen the Assacenes, Alexander offered the 7,000 Indian mercenaries defending the city safe conduct, and then slaughtered them along with their wives and children when they refused to join his army and fight their fellow countrymen. The population of one valley destroyed their own villages and fled from what they saw as barbaric invaders. Their impression was confirmed when Alexander's men committed what seems to have been an accidental act of sacrilege. One cold

Alexander's troops conquering the Indus fortress

night, their campfires set ablaze a wood where coffins – seemingly belonging to some exotic sect of Parsees – were hung from the trees, burning them.

During this campaign Alexander paid a visit to Nysa, where the god Dionysus was venerated. It is thought that Dionysus was associated with the Hindu god Shiva, who is the restorer as well as the destroyer, the symbol of sensuality as well as the great ascetic. When Alexander approached, the people of Nysa sent their chief, Acuphis, out to meet him with a delegation of 30 distinguished citizens. Apparently when they entered Alexander's tent, they found him sitting there dusty and dishevelled from his travels, still wearing his armour, with his helmet on his head and his spear in his hand. The sight of this barbaric figure scared them so much that they prostrated themselves on the ground and lay there for a long time without uttering a word. Eventually Alexander told them to get up and not to be alarmed. They did and Acuphis began to address the king.

'Sire, it is the request of the people of Nysa that you show your reverence for Dionysus by leaving them free and independent,' he said. 'For when Dionysus, after his conquest of the Indians, was on his way homeward towards the Greek sea, he founded this city as a memorial of his long journey and his victory, leaving to inhabit it those of his men who were no longer fit for service – who were also his priests. He did but as you have done; for you too founded Alexandria-in-the-Caucasus and Alexandria in Egypt and many other cities as well, and will found yet more hereafter, in that you will have surpassed the achievements of Dionysus.'

Alexander was pleased with what Acuphis had to say. Again he was rivalling Dionysus and would soon be surpassing him. He knew that his Macedonian troops would be happy to share his hardships a little longer, if they knew they were in competition with Dionysus. So he granted the people of Nysa their freedom and autonomy.[115] Meanwhile, in Nysa, Alexander's men crowned themselves with ivy and held a ten-day Bacchic drinking festival. According to the Greek writer Philostratus, Alexander and his men climbed to the summit of the mountain of Nysa and visited a shrine of Dionysus, which Dionysus had founded in honour of himself. 'There were sickles and winepresses and they are dedicated to Dionysus, as if to one who gathers grapes, all made of gold and silver. And the image resembled a youthful Indian, and was carved out of polished white stone.'[116]

When Alexander reached the Indus in March 326, the people fled to a high mountain fortress known as Aornus. This is probably the Greek transliteration of the Sanskrit *avarana*, which means 'hiding place'. This was a fortress that stood on the great massif of Pir-Sar rising 5,000 feet above a bend in the Indus. According to local legend, not even the god Krishna – who the Macedonians identified with Alexander's legendary ancestor Heracles – had been able to take this stronghold. Although there was no military necessity to take Aornus, the fact that Heracles had failed to do so was enough of an incentive for Alexander. He contacted Hephaestion who was some way downstream to send the catapults and artillery. They were then hauled up the 8,721 feet of the nearby Una-Sir massif. Then they had to be moved across a wooden bridge Alexander's engineers had constructed over a ravine to a mountaintop that overlooked Pir-Sar. The defenders fled. The message was clear to both Indian and Macedonian alike. The Indians were facing a god more powerful than Krishna: Alexander had succeeded where Heracles had failed.

In April, the two Macedonian armies joined up near modern Attock, where Perdiccas and Hephaestion had built a pontoon bridge of local boats – a great feat as, even in the dry season, the Indus is seldom less than a mile across. Alexander appointed Nicanor, a Macedonian, as satrap of Gandara and the western Punjab. Then the Macedonian army crossed the Indus and reached Taxila, where Alexander was greeted by king Ambhi, the rajah of

Taxila, at the head of his forces. Ambhi had invited Alexander's help in his battle against his rival Porus, but the sight of the rajah's army in full battle array led Alexander to fear that he was falling into a trap. He was particularly afraid of Indian war-elephants. His cavalry was useless against them as horses go mad with fright near elephants, unless especially trained.[117] Alexander sounded the trumpets and ordered his men into battle formation. Seeing this, Ambhi rode ahead with a small cavalry escort and surrendered himself and his army to Alexander, who immediately reinstated him as rajah of Taxila, though he took the precaution of providing him with a Macedonian military governor.

Over the next three days, Ambhi lavished gifts on Alexander. But Alexander never allowed himself to be outdone – even in generosity. He returned everything that Ambhi had given him and gave the rajah a wardrobe of Persian robes, 30 horses, gold and silver ornaments, and 1,000 talents in cash.[118] Again this caused dissent among Alexander's troops, who thought he was giving away spoils that should have come to them. But Alexander realised that he was up against a far more formidable foe, Porus, the ruler of Paurava in what is now the Punjab. He needed to be sure of the support of Ambhi and his generosity also persuaded Abisares, the rajah of neighbouring Kashmir, to submit.[119]

The discovery of crocodiles in the Indus and a variety of bean seen in Egypt growing along its banks caused some speculation that this river was the head water of the Nile. Alexander encouraged the idea, hoping that his troops would feel that they were closer to home than was actually the case. But locals soon dispelled the false impression.[120]

At Taxila, Alexander also met Brahmin sages. He always liked to meet philosophers and wise men, and visited the meadow where they gathered to discuss philosophy. But when he turned up with his army, the sages' only response was to stamp their feet. Through an interpreter, Alexander asked what this bizarre behaviour meant. This was their reply: 'King Alexander, every man can possess only so much of the earth's surface as this we are standing on. You are but human like the rest of us, save that you are always busy and up to no good, travelling so many miles from your home, a nuisance to yourself and to others. Ah well! You will soon be dead, and then you will own just as much of this earth as will suffice to bury you.'

'Alexander expressed his approval of these sage words,' notes Arrian, adding the comment: 'but in point of fact his conduct was always the exact opposite of what he then professed to admire.'[121]

The Brahmins were honoured as advisers and counsellors and, in the markets, were given anything they needed, free. They ate standing up and lay on the ground in the open both on the hottest day and in the monsoon rains. Sometimes they would stand motionless on one leg for hours, holding aloft a heavy weight.[122] Alexander was particularly impressed by the powers of endurance of a sect of fanatics who went about naked, and wanted one of them to join his court as an adviser. But their leader Dandamis refused to work for Alexander or to permit any of his pupils to do so.

'If you, my lord, are the son of god,' he said, 'why – so am I. I want nothing from you, for what I have suffices. I perceive, more-over, that the men you lead get no good from their worldwide wandering over land and sea, and that of their many journeyings there will be no end. I desire nothing that you can give me; I fear no exclusion from any blessings which may perhaps be yours. India, with the fruits of her soil in due season, is enough for me while I live; and when I die, I shall be rid of my poor body – my unseemly housemate.'

These words convinced Alexander that Dandamis was, in the truest sense, a free man and he made no attempt to compel him. Another Indian teacher, however, a man named Kalyana, known as Calanus in Greek, did agree to join Alexander. The others con-demned him as a slave to fleshly lusts for having chosen to renounce the bliss of asceticism and to serve an earthly master instead of god.[123] Calanus answered them, saying that he had already completed the 40 years of discipline that he had promised.[124]

It also seems that Calanus was greatly amused by Alexander when he first saw him. Calanus was lying naked on some stones at the time and laughed at the cloak, broad-brimmed hat and boots Alexander was wearing and said: 'In olden times the world was full of barley-meal and wheaten-meal, as now of dust; and fountains then flowed, some with water, others with milk and likewise with honey, and others with wine, and some with olive oil; but, by reason of his gluttony and luxury, man fell into arrogance beyond bounds. Zeus, hating this state of things, destroyed everything and appointed for man a life of toil. And when self-control and the other virtues in general reappeared, there came again an abundance of blessings. But the condition of man is already close to satiety and arrogance, and there is danger of destruction of everything in existence.'

Calanus then told Alexander that, if he wished to learn, he should take off his clothes, lie down naked on the stones next to him and listen to his teachings. When Alexander hesitated another sage named Mandanis mocked Calanus for trying to teach 'the only philosopher in arms that he ever saw' and told Alexander that the only thing a man like him, who had 'the power of persuading the willing and forcing the unwilling', needed to learn was self-control.[125] Alexander did not lie down. Instead, Calanus accepted Alexander's invitation to dine at his table, but insisted on eating standing up.

Victory on the Hydaspes
326

While Ambhi and Abisares submitted to Alexander, Porus, king of Paurava, refused to become a vassal and sent a message saying that he would meet Alexander in battle at the river Hydaspes – the modern-day Jhelum. He may have thought that he was safe as the river, which marked the frontier of his kingdom, was swollen by the melting of the mountain snows and the monsoon rains. What's more he had Alexander's small force of 30,000 men – only half of whom were Macedonians – heavily outnumbered. According to Alexander's intelligence reports Porus had 50,000 infantrymen and 3,000-4,000 cavalry, along with 300 war-chariots and 200 elephants.[126] And when Abisares learnt that Porus was prepared to fight Alexander, he changed sides and marched towards the Hydaspes with reinforcements.

Alexander could not afford to let these two forces meet up. He had to move quickly. He only had time to mobilise half of his army for the initial march to the east. There was no time to build boats to cross the Hydaspes, so the ships used to make the pontoon bridge across the Indus were cut up, transported overland by cart then reassembled. Meanwhile his troops marched towards the Hydaspes in the monsoon. Despite the torrential rain, they covered the 110 miles from Taxila in just two days.[127]

Haranpur was one of the few places where the Hydaspes could be forded and Porus waited there on the southern bank. When Alexander arrived, the river was swollen with monsoon rain and was nearly half a mile wide. Across the river, he could see Porus's immense army and squadrons of elephants, 85 strong, trumpeting and marching back and forth. Even if crossing the river were possible, it would be suicidal to attempt a landing on the opposite bank against such opposition. And Alexander's scouts soon told him that all other likely crossing points were also held in strength.[128]

Alexander publicly declared that he intended to camp on the northern bank of the Hydaspes until the rains stopped and the river became fordable again. He brought in wagons of grain and other supplies to bolster this impression. Meanwhile he also made a great show of preparing for battle. The infantry would march up and down, squelching through the thick red mud. Cavalry detachments would gallop from one outpost to another and assault craft would take to the waters, occasionally landing on the small islands near Haranpur which could serve as a bridgehead.[129] When no actual attack materialised, Porus began to ignore the Macedonian activity – which was exactly what Alexander had intended. Meanwhile his cavalry scouted the river up as far as Jalalpur. Some 17 miles upstream they found what Alexander was looking for: a wooded island in the centre of the river with narrow channels on either side and a deep ravine on the northern bank of the river where men and boats could be hidden in preparation for an attack.[130]

While Alexander planned his attack, he spent more time and effort trying to confuse Porus. At night, his men lit fires over a wide area and created a great commotion, while Ptolemy led a large detachment of cavalry 'up and down the bank of the river, making as much noise as possible – shots, war-cries and every sort of clatter and shindy which might be supposed to precede an attempted crossing'.[131] This prompted Porus into action once more. He brought up his elephants and deployed his cavalry at places where landings seemed imminent. But again there was no attack. All this wasted effort merely demoralised Porus's troops and he began to ignore movements on the other bank again.

By this time Abisares was just 50 miles away with 'an army little smaller than that of Porus'.[132] Alexander had to attack immediately. Despite his diversionary tactics, he knew that, once an attack had started, Porus would know of it quickly from his outlook posts – which were within earshot of each other[133] – and counter attack. Alexander's only hope lay in dividing Porus's forces long enough to get a substantial force across the river.

Alexander ordered that the main body of the army, along with non-combatants and the baggage train, were to stay at the Haranpur camp under the command of Craterus. Alexander's pavilion was to remain there in a conspicuous position and a double would appear every so often wearing a royal cloak 'in order to give the impression the king himself was encamped on that part of the bank'.[134]

Meanwhile Alexander hid with a crack assault force of 5,000 cavalry and at least 10,000 infantrymen in the ravine opposite Admana Island – the island his scouts had found – ready to cross the river. A second force was stationed at a ford halfway between Haranpur and Admana Island, with instructions to cross only once battle had been joined.[135] Craterus's main force was told not to attempt a crossing unless Porus had left his position to attack Alexander and there were no elephants left behind to defend the ford or he was sure that 'Porus was in retreat and the Greeks victorious'.[136] This deployment meant that whichever way Porus moved he would leave himself open to attack from the rear. It was a brilliant plan and has been studied by military strategists ever since.[137] But on the day it almost failed.

The night before the attack, there was a thunderstorm. Several of Alexander's men were killed by lightning strikes, but the thunder masked the sound of his troops embarking.[138] By dawn, the Royal Squadron of the Companions, three cavalry brigades, two phalanx battalions and the Guards Brigade under Alexander's top commanders, along with archers, horse-archers and cavalry units from Turkestan and Bactria – some 15,000 to 16,000 men in all – were sailing down the northern channel alongside

Admana Island. But the moment they passed the western tip of the island, they were spotted and a messenger galloped off at top speed to inform Porus.[139] It was then that everything went wrong. Alexander put ashore on what he took to be the southern bank of the Hydaspes. In fact, he had landed on another long, narrow island. His reconnaissance may have been faulty, or the heavy rain that night might have created a new channel separating this island from the riverbank.

The bulk of his men were ashore before Alexander realised the mistake and there was no time to get them back on the boats. They would have to ford across the river in full flood. The horses crossed with little more than their heads showing, while the infantrymen, weighed down with heavy armour, somehow struggled to shore. They quickly formed up behind a screen of horse-archers.[140]

Porus could not be sure that this landing party was Alexander's main force and with all the activity that Craterus was creating in the Haranpur camp, he dared not move his own main force to counter it. Instead he sent his son with a small force of 2,000 cavalry and 120 battle-chariots. This was too little too late. Macedonia's finest cavalry units were already ashore. They were more than a match for the Indian horsemen whose chariots bogged down in the mud. Porus's son was killed and his Indian troops fled, leaving 400 dead.[141]

Even when news of his son's death reached Porus, he could not be sure that the crossing was not a feint, especially as Alexander's victory in the skirmish had led Craterus to begin preparations to cross the river. Eventually, he left a holding force with elephants to keep Craterus at bay and advanced towards Alexander with some 20,000 infantry, 2,000 cavalry, 180 battle-chariots and 130 elephants.

Porus was no bad tactician himself and selected as the battle ground a flat, sandy plain, free from mud where his elephants, battle chariots and cavalry could manoeuvre easily. The exact site has

not been identified, but it is probably near a village called Sikandarpur – 'Alexanderville' in Hindi, though that name is not uncommon in the Punjab.[142] Porus drew up his infantry behind a line of elephants with his cavalry on the flanks behind the battle-chariots.[143] The line stretched for four miles.

Alexander had moved fast. By the time he arrived on the battlefield, his cavalry was two miles ahead of the infantry. He could not attack the infantry behind its screen of elephants, so he would have to take on the Indian cavalry. He came up with an ingenious plan. First, 1,000 mounted archers knocked out Porus's battle chariots. Then he divided his cavalry in two and led a charge against the cavalry on the Indian left with a force just small enough for Porus to think that he could destroy it with an all-out counter-attack. The remaining two divisions under Coenus were to circle out of sight around the Indian right wing.

Porus fell into the trap. Observing the battle from a howdah on the back of a war-elephant, he estimated that he could destroy Alexander's assault on his left if he attacked it with all his cavalry. He ordered the cavalry on his right to move round to the left to join the battle. Coenus had strict instructions not to break cover until the Indian cavalry on the right had moved. The moment they did, he followed, attacking them from the rear as they reached the

other end of the line. As the Indian cavalry turned back to face Coenus, Alexander pressed home his frontal assault.[144] Alexander had caught Porus's cavalry in a fore-and-aft attack.

By now, the Macedonian infantry was on the field. They attacked the centre with javelins and bows and arrows. They were in luck. The Indian bows, positioned behind the line of elephants, packed a powerful punch but they were heavy and had to be rested on the ground, and the storm-soaked battlefield rendered them ineffective.[145] Alexander's men had also figured out how to deal with the war-elephants. Archers surrounded them and shot their mahouts, while infantrymen threw spears and javelins at vulnerable parts of the animal, hacked at their feet with axes and slashed their trunks with scimitars. Even so, many Macedonians were trampled underfoot, impaled on tusks or picked up by the elephants' trunks and dashed to the ground. At the same time, the phalanx faced the Indian infantry. But the long Macedonian *sarissa* (a kind of pike) proved just as effective as it had against the Greeks.

The phalanx's attack was so effective that it forced the Indian line back until the elephants trampled the infantrymen behind them.[146] Porus led one last elephant charge, which failed, and soon the elephants 'began to back away, slowly, like ships going astern, and with nothing worse than trumpetings'.[147] The Indians were now ringed by Alexander's cavalry. He ordered the phalanx and the Guards Brigade to 'lock shields and move up in a solid mass'.[148] The rest was butchery. Indian deaths were put at anywhere between 12,000 and 23,000. Both Porus's sons were killed. Even those who managed to break through Alexander's cavalry were slaughtered by Craterus who had now crossed the river with fresh units.[149]

Porus himself was injured by a javelin in the right shoulder. Weak from loss of blood, he left the battlefield. Alexander sent Ambhi after him. But Porus regarded Ambhi as a turncoat and tried to run him through with a lance. Eventually, others were sent and brought Porus back to Alexander. According to Arrian: 'When they met, Alexander reined in his horse and looked at his adversary with admiration. He was a magnificent figure of a man, over seven feet high and of great personal beauty; his bearing had lost none of its pride; his air was of one brave man meeting another, of a king in the presence of a king with whom he had fought honourably for his kingdom.'

When Alexander asked him how he wanted to be treated, Porus said: 'Like a king.' If there was anything else he wanted for himself, Alexander said, he only had to ask. 'Everything,' Porus replied, 'is contained in that one request.'[150] The two men had an instinctive understanding and Alexander made Porus satrap of Paurava.

Porus (died 317) was the king of the eastern Punjab. The Greek/Latin name Porus is a rendering of the Indian Puru, which is the name of a tribe known in that region from ancient Hindu Vedic times. They were the traditional rulers of the kingdom Paurava, which extended from the river Hydaspes – the modern Jhelum – to the Hydraotis – the Ravi. Little is known of him before his defeat at the hands of Alexander in 326. Alexander made him satrap of his former kingdom, later giving him additional territories to the north. After the death of Alexander, Porus was still recognised as defender of the eastern border of Alexander's empire and he survived its subsequent division. But in 317, some of the eastern provinces' satraps rebelled and one of their leaders had Porus killed in order to procure his elephants. Porus's sons were already dead so there was no obvious successor and the Pauravan forces were effectively neutralised. Sandrocottos – or Chandragupta – the king of Magadha to the east was able to conquer the Indus valley, ending the Macedonian presence in India less than ten years after Alexander's invasion.

Casualties among Alexander's men were high too. Losses were recorded at 280 cavalry and over 700 infantry.[151] However, these seem to be an underestimate and experts put the figure closer to 4,000.[152] Bucephalus had been injured and died. Alexander gave his charger a state funeral and named the new city built on the site of the battle Bucephalia. Another new city founded nearby was called Nicaea, which means 'city of victory'.

To the east of Porus's kingdom lay the kingdom of Magadha in the Ganges valley. Alexander now aimed to add it to his empire. After that he intended to march on all the way to the shores of the Eastern Ocean – the Bay of Bengal – which he told his men was not far away.[153] Even before the end of the monsoon, they started their march eastwards, crossing the Chenab and Ravi rivers in early July. A town called Sangala, near Amritsar, was besieged, taken and destroyed.[154] But more than 1,200 of Alexander's men were wounded in the action.[155]

By now, the Macedonians had little stomach for fighting. They were no longer the eager youths that had left Pella eight years before. They had marched over 17,000 miles and had fought countless battles and sieges. Few had survived unscathed. Their arms and armour were worn out and their Macedonian clothes had long since been thrown away.

While Alexander and his generals were fêted by Indian dignitaries, the soldiers were left out in the rain, sleeping in hammocks in trees to avoid being bitten by the numerous snakes. As they neared the Hyphasis river – the Vipasha in Sanskrit, the modern Beas – they left the hills behind and got their first clear view across the vast plain on the other side, with the great ramparts of the western Himalayas rising up in the distance.[156] Plainly, the army was nowhere near the Eastern Ocean. Rumours circulated that, 12 days march beyond the Hyphasis, lay an even greater river – presumably the Sutlej – which marked the frontier of a warlike nation whose army boasted 4,000 fighting elephants.[157]

Alexander was still gung ho. How much geographical knowledge he had of what lay ahead is not known. But to reach even the most westerly tributary of the Ganges, the Yamuna, meant crossing 200 miles of the north Indian desert. Then from the Yamuna down the Ganges to the ocean was another 2,000 miles.

His men were now on the brink of mutiny. They had originally left Macedonia to punish Persia. They had conquered it, only to see their king take on Persian ways. Then they had invaded India, taking kingdoms that had once been part of the Achaemenid empire in the time of Darius I. But they knew that the Hyphasis marked the eastern frontier of Darius I's empire and the furthest extent of what had ever been Persian.[158] They now feared that Alexander aimed to march them on to the end of the world.

He tried to placate them by allowing them to loot the surrounding countryside and offering their wives free monthly rations and a child allowance.[159] But bribery did not work this time. When his men returned from their looting spree, he gave a stirring speech about the glory that awaited them to the east and ordered them to cross the river. They refused. They did nothing loudly or aggressively mutinous. They merely stood there in a sullen silence and refused to budge.

Alexander called a meeting of his officers and tried to talk them around. Soon they would reach the Ganges and the Eastern Ocean, he said. Why turn back when their goal was so near at hand? Many of his men believed that they had begun their long campaign to punish the Persians. But Alexander made it all too clear that he had passed any need of reasons: *For a man who is a man*, he said, *work, in my belief, if it is directed to noble ends, has no object beyond itself*.[160]

When he finished his speech there was silence. Since the murder of Cleitus, his officers knew better than to oppose him openly. But after he had several times invited them to respond, Coenus spoke up. He had been one of Parmenio's officers, was old and near the end of his life. He told Alexander that his army was worn out. Many of his men were already dead, killed by disease or in battle. The survivors were 'a small remnant broken in health, their old vigour and determination gone', who craved just one thing – to return home before they died. 'If there is one thing above all others a successful man should know,' Coenus told Alexander, 'it is when to stop.'[161]

Annoyed at Coenus's plain speaking, Alexander dismissed the meeting. He called his officers together again the following day and told them angrily that he was going on, if necessary without them. He would not force any Macedonians to follow him against their will, he said. Those who wanted to go home could do so and tell the people of Macedonia that they had *deserted their king in the midst of his enemies*. Then he withdrew to his tent and refused to see anyone for three days.[162]

Alexander had used this ploy before. He expected his men to change their minds, but they did not. They were annoyed by his show of temper and they did not care if he starved himself to death. Before, they had been in a hostile land and needed him to lead them. But now the situation was reversed. He needed them, while they were perfectly capable of making their way back to Macedonia without him. According to Ptolemy, Alexander emerged from his tent after three days, still determined to go on. He offered sacrifice in the hope of obtaining favourable omens. It was a face-saving exercise. The omens turned out to be bad, so he called together the Companions and told the army that he had decided to turn back.

'At this there arose a loud shout such as you would expect from a large and joyful multitude, and many of them wept,' Arrian wrote. 'Some drew near the royal tent and called for many blessings on Alexander, since he had allowed himself to be defeated by them and them alone.'[163]

Alexander then divided the army into 12 parts and gave them orders to build 12 altars to the 12 Olympian gods to thank them for having brought him victorious so far. These huge altars were also designed to show that Alexander's army had been 'men of huge stature, displaying the strength of giants'.[164] Assorted siege engines and other bits of military equipment – even dining couches – were left there. According to the Greek writer Philostratus, the Indians erected a brass obelisk, carrying the inscription: 'Alexander stopped here.'[165]

Turning Homeward
326 to 325

Alexander decided not to return to Macedonia the way he had come. It might look as if he had suffered a defeat. Instead he would make his way down to the Arabian Sea and return via the Persian Gulf. First he marched his army back to the Jhelum, leaving all the territory he had conquered up to the Beas in the hands of Porus. This left Porus more powerful that he had been before his defeat at the battle of Hydaspes. Craterus had already assembled a fleet of over 1,800 vessels on the river. The larger vessels had been built from timber felled in the Himalayas. The rest had been commandeered. Skilled seamen from the Phoenician, Carian, Cypriot and Egyptian units accompanying Alexander were employed to sail them.

Alexander was now running short of money. He had not acquired much loot during his incursion into India and bribes and the expense of living the life of an eastern potentate had emptied his coffers. He never had less than 60 or 70 officers at dinner and the mess bill alone came to 10,000 drachmas a day. So the ships were paid for by a number of wealthy men known as 'trierarchs', who were rewarded with prestige – a system employed by the Athenians to build their navy.

Though Alexander had to raise money for his fleet, he could still order reinforcements from other parts of his empire. 6,000 cavalry and 30,000 infantrymen arrived from Greece, Thrace and Babylon, bringing with them much-needed medicine and 25,000 new suits of armour, inlaid with precious metal. When these were issued to his men, Alexander ordered them to burn their old equipment, which was now in an appalling state.[166]

The one thing the new troops did not bring with them was money. Alexander began to suspect that Harpalus, the quartermaster he had left at Ecbatana with the bullion looted from Persepolis, was not dealing honestly with him. In fact, Harpalus was spending Alexander's money to indulge his passion for horticulture. He imported expensive plants and shrubs from Greece, finding that only the ivy failed to flourish.[167] He also imported a beautiful Athenian courtesan and spent 200 talents to build monuments to her in Athens and Babylon. A second Athenian courtesan, named Glycera, was set up in a palace in Tarsus, furnished with a golden crown and spoken of as the 'Queen of Babylon'. Visitors were required to prostrate themselves before her: Harpalus was taking *proskynesis* even further than Alexander himself.[168]

Harpalus earned himself honorary Athenian citizenship by sending Athens a huge consignment of wheat during a famine and began to mint silver coins without reference to Alexander. When news of Harpalus's excesses reached Alexander, he refused to believe what he was told and jailed the messengers. But then a detailed report from the historian Theopompus of Chios convinced him. There was nothing that he could do about Harpalus until he returned to Babylonia, but he certainly knew of the problem. At the festival of Dionysus in December 326, Harpalus, Glycera and their Athenian connections were lampooned in a satirical sketch known as the *Agen*, fragments of which survive. According to tradition, Alexander wrote it himself.[169] At the very least, he must have given his approval.

Alexander now had 100,000 men to take down the river. He made sacrifices and poured libations from a golden chalice on the prow of his ship. These were to propitiate the water gods, Oceanus, Poseidon and the Nereids. Offerings were also made to the rivers his fleet would sail down, the Jhelum (Hydaspes), Chenab and Indus, and his ancestors Heracles and Zeus Ammon. Then in early November 326, the fleet cast off from Jalalpur.

Despite the number of ships, only 8,000 men – including the Companion Cavalry and the Guards Brigade – were carried on board. The rest were marched down the banks in columns commanded by Craterus and Hephaestion. A third column under Philip, the newly appointed satrap of Taxila, accompanied the baggage train, which brought up the rear.

The navy was under the command of the Cretan admiral Nearchus, who wrote an account of the voyage called the *Indike*. The fleet travelled with up to 40 ships abreast down the Jhelum, which was two and a half miles wide. They sailed just five miles a day, disembarking frequently. On the journey Alexander passed the time with readings of a glamorised account of the battle of Hydaspes composed by Aristobulus, in which he was said to have brought down Porus's war elephant with a single javelin thrust.[170]

The fleet had been travelling for ten days, when it reached the confluence of the Jhelum and Chenab. In the turbulent water there several ships sank and many men lost their lives. Alexander's flagship nearly foundered and Alexander, who could not swim, had to be rescued.[171]

In January 325, Alexander learnt that the Oxydracae – the Kshatriya or Kshudraka Hindu warrior caste – and the Malli – or Malavas, who lived around modern Multan – were mobilising to block his path to the Arabian Sea. They had 100,000 men under arms and 900 war-chariots.[172] Faced with the prospect of fighting once more, Alexander's men were soon on the point of mutiny. Alexander assured them that the people ahead were not warlike and the ocean was now so close that they could smell the sea. In fact, it was over 400 miles away and even the prospect of reaching the sea did not offer any reassurance: the men believed its depths to be teeming with sea monsters[173] and morale remained low.

Alexander tried to inspire his men with his customary panache, winning a notable victory after a 50-mile forced march across a waterless desert before dawn.[174] Several Mallian towns, including modern-day Kamalia and Talamba, were captured and their inhabitants slaughtered.[175] During the siege of the capital of the Malli, modern Multan, a soothsayer – perhaps sensing the troops' reluctance – warned Alexander against continuing the attack as the omens indicated that his life was in danger. Alexander ignored his advice. *If anyone interrupted you while you were about your professional business, I have no doubt you would find it both tactless and annoying, correct?* Alexander said. *Well, my business – my vital business – is the capture of this citadel, and I don't intend to let any superstitious crackpot stand in my way.*[176]

Alexander called for scaling ladders, but his men refused to climb them. So he climbed up alone, holding a light shield over his head. At the top he killed the defenders who barred his way, then stood alone on top of the battlements – the perfect target for any archer. When his men begged him to come down, he jumped down inside the citadel. With his back to the wall and one side protected by a tree, he took on all-comers. He was soon joined by his shield-bearer Peucestas, carrying the sacred shield taken from Troy, a bodyguard named Leonnatus and Abreas, a highly decorated guards officer.

Alexander's action was calculated to inspire the rest of his men to follow. But when they did, so many of them tried to climb the ladders at once that they broke under the weight. The Macedonians then stormed the gate with axes and mattocks as missiles rained down on them from the ramparts. Abreas fell, shot in the face, and Alexander was struck by an arrow that pierced his breastplate and lodged in his chest. Meanwhile the Macedonians scaled the walls using improvised pitons and, finally, broke down the gate. Inside, they massacred every man, woman and child, while the injured Alexander was carried away on his shield. The rumour quickly spread that he was dead or dying.[177]

The arrow in his chest was barbed and difficult to remove. Perdiccas had to cut it out using his sword as no doctor could be found, or none who was willing to risk killing the king. Alexander lost a great deal of blood and lapsed into a coma. For a week he hovered between life and death.[178]

At the Macedonian camp, which was now at the junction of the Chenab and the Ravi rivers, there was consternation. At the Beas, the Macedonians could have done without Alexander and simply returned to Greece the way they had come through lands previously pacified. But now they were surrounded by hostile tribes greatly heartened by the news that Alexander seemed likely to die.[179] There were even rumours that 3,000 Greek mercenaries who had been settled in Bactria had rebelled and were heading for home.[180]

The moment Alexander regained consciousness he wrote a letter to his troops, telling them that he was alive. They did not believe it and dismissed the letter as a forgery. Only a personal appearance would do. Alexander had to be carried down river to the camp on a day bed mounted high above the deck of a boat so that both the Indians and his own men could see him. From a distance, many believed that the recumbent figure was dead. But when he came in sight of the Macedonian camp, Alexander managed a wave and a great cheer went up.

During the banquet given to celebrate Alexander's recovery, he backed the Macedonian veteran Corragus against the Athenian boxer Dioxippus in a fight. Dioxippus had earlier told Alexander that the blood that flowed from his wound was divine ichor – that is, the fluid that flowed in the veins of the gods. While Corragus wore full armour and carried both sword and spear, Dioxippus fought naked, armed only with a club. Even so Dioxippus finished off Corragus in a matter of seconds. Alexander, angered by the damage to the prestige of Macedonia, stormed from the party. After that Dioxippus's life was made a misery. He was accused of stealing a gold chalice that had been planted on him. Eventually he committed suicide. Typically Alexander was racked with remorse, but only when it was too late to do anything about it.[182]

When the boat reached the shore, a stretcher was waiting for Alexander. He sent it away. Instead, with iron resolution, he climbed on a horse and rode into camp to the cheers of his men in a blizzard of flowers. Alexander, it seemed to friend and foe alike, was invincible and immortal. The Malli surrendered and Oxydracae gave up without a fight. However, Alexander was all too mortal and suffered from the effects of his wound for the rest of his short life.[181]

Alexander being rescued by a friend.
Mosaic in Pella, Greece

As Alexander moved on, he made his father-in-law Oxyartes the satrap of the Hindu Kush, while a Macedonian named Peithon was given Lower India. He built a number of new towns with dockyards, suggesting that he wanted to develop trade with the Indus valley. It took him another five months to reach the sea. During that period he fought a series of bloody battles in a holy war largely instigated by Brahmin priests. He hanged any Brahmin that fell into his hands, reserving crucifixion for civil leaders that opposed him. He asked one Brahmin why he had encouraged his king to revolt. His reply was: 'Because I wished him to live with honour or die with honour.' This bloodthirsty repression simply stored up resentment for the future. By 300 every Macedonian garrison in the Punjab had been slaughtered.[183]

In July 325, Alexander reached Pattala at the head of the delta of the Indus. The inhabitants had heard of Alexander's slaughter of the populace inland and evacuated the city. Alexander had to beg them to return as he needed labour to build more dockyards there. Hephaestion was left there to supervise the building work while Alexander sailed on down the westerly channel of the Indus delta on a reconnaissance trip. Nearing the sea, the fleet was hit by a storm and Alexander took shelter in a side channel, only to find his ships grounded by the outgoing tide – a phenomenon unfamiliar to his seamen, used to the smaller tides of the Mediterranean. Imagining that they were stranded permanently, his men wandered off across the mudflats and found themselves menaced by huge crabs. They were taken completely by surprise when a huge tidal bore refloated the boats, damaging some of them.

When he reached the sea, Alexander set up altars to Oceanus and his wife Tethys and sacrificed a bull to Poseidon. Then he explored the coast and sailed back up river via the easterly channel of the Indus delta, which gave him better shelter from the monsoon winds.

With the fleet now ready for the journey along the coast to the Persian Gulf, Alexander divided his army. Craterus was sent with about a quarter of the army and the elephants overland via the province of Carmania to Persia. Alexander and the rest of his men would march along the coast, digging wells as they went to supply fresh water, while the navy kept pace to supply them with provisions as they went. This was the strategy adopted by Xerxes when he invaded Greece in 480BC.

Alexander knew it was going to be a hazardous journey. For several hundred miles the Makran Coast is a barren desert, nothing but rocks, scoured by wind-blown red dust. According to legend, Queen Semiramis and Cyrus the Great had both attempted this route. Queen Semiramis got through with no more than 20 survivors. Cyrus lost a whole army, emerging with less than seven men. Once more Alexander was spurred on by the idea that he would succeed where all others had failed.[184]

Things did not start well as Alexander had no money to purchase supplies. He was reduced to borrowing from friends. When he asked his chief secretary Eumenes for 300 talents, Eumenes said he could only spare 100. So Alexander set fire to Eumenes' tent and watched while he rescued his hidden valuables. Alexander obtained over 1,000 talents in gold and silver in this way, with which he bought grain and salt fish.[185] However, the fire also destroyed many of the records of the expedition.[186] Before he set off, Alexander founded a new city named Rhambacia and left Apollophanes as satrap of the region with Leonnatus as military governor.

Alexander started out with a number of punitive raids against the local tribes. The Greeks nicknamed one stone-age tribe, Ichthyophagi or the 'Fish-Eaters'. They were hairy all over, with matted locks and long, uncut fingernails. They wore shark-skins or animal pelts and lived in houses made from the rib cages of beached whales. Even their cattle were fed on fishmeal and their meat had a distinctly fishy taste. It was impossible to get other provisions out of them as nothing grew in the area except for thorn and tamarisk.

Further along the coast, the mountains came right down to the sea and Alexander had to make a detour inland through the Gedrosian desert. His men would have to march up to 75 miles between brackish wells and it was so hot that they were forced to move largely at night. When they did find water, thirst-crazed men would dive in, in full armour. Many died from over-drinking; others from heatstroke.

At one point during this march, a helmet full of muddy water dredged from a gully was offered to Alexander. As there was no more water to be had, Alexander thanked the donor and tipped it out onto the sand, determined to share the hardship of his men. According to Arrian: 'So extraordinary was the effect of this action that the water wasted by Alexander was as good as a drink for every man in the army.'[187]

Boots filled with sand and wagons bogged down in the dunes. Where there was vegetation, it was home to poisonous snakes. Prickly cucumbers, which looked like they might yield moisture, sprayed a blinding juice into the eyes of those who picked them. Pack animals died foaming at the mouth after eating poisonous leaves, while men choked to death from eating too many unripe dates. Alexander turned a blind eye when sealed stores were broken open surreptitiously and pack animals slaughtered and eaten. Men dropped along the wayside from exhaustion.

Although the region was poor in food and water, it was rich in myrrh and spikenard. Phoenician merchants accompanying the column loaded their mules with these valuable aromatics and the advancing army, despite its other privations, reeked of the most glorious perfume.

One night the baggage train camped in a dry wadi. A flash-flood in the darkness washed away the baggage, the tents – including Alexander's royal pavilion – many of the remaining pack animals and almost all the women and children. Most of his men escaped drowning, but were left with nothing but what they stood up in. Some had even lost their weapons. Then a sandstorm obscured the landmarks and the army got lost, wandering further and further from the coast. When Alexander realised what had happened, he set off with a small cavalry detachment southwards, towards the sea. Reaching a beach, they dug down in the shingle there and found fresh water. For the next week, the army marched along the coast, finding water wherever they dug for it. Sixty days after they had left the Indus delta, they reached safety at the Gedrosian capital of Pura. Of the 85,000 who had set out – most of them non-combatants – less than 25,000 survived. Even the crack Companion Cavalry lost 700 of its men.[188]

'So it was that Alexander, his pride soaring above the human plane, . . . decided to imitate the god [Dionysus's] procession. . . . He gave orders for villages along his route to be strewn with flowers and garlands, and for bowls full of wine and other vessels of extraordinary size to be set out on the thresholds of houses. Then he had wagons covered with planks (so that they would hold a greater number of soldiers) and rigged out like tents, some with white curtains, others with costly material. The friends and the royal company went in front, heads wreathed with various kinds of flowers woven into garlands, with the notes of the flute heard at one point, the tones of the lyre at another. The army joined the revels in wagons decorated as far as individual means allowed, and with their finest arms hung around them. . . . In this way, the army spent seven days on a drunken march, an easy prey if the vanquished races had only had the courage to challenge riotous drinkers.'

QUINTUS CURTIUS RUFUS[189]

But the food stocks at Pura were soon running low. None of the food that Alexander had ordered his satraps to send arrived and Nearchus and the fleet were nowhere to be seen. Alexander suspected treachery and sent a letter to the satrap in Rhambacia, Apollophanes, deposing him – only to learn from Leonnatus soon after that he had been killed by rebellious tribesmen. He also received news from Craterus, telling him that he had suppressed an uprising in Arachosia and was sending the seditious Persian nobles to him in chains. Alexander pressed on into Carmania where he met up with Craterus at the end of 325. The ordeal was over. The satraps of Drangiana and Parthia had sent racing camels bringing food. The harvest was in and the winter rains had started. This was a time for celebration. Alexander dressed himself as Dionysus, and the army went on a drunken spree that lasted for seven days.

The Purge of Persia
324

Many of the officers and satraps Alexander had left behind in Persia thought that Alexander would never return from the east. They heard of the grievous wound he had received at the hands of the Malli, and, thinking he might die, began to make provision for their own future. When Alexander had been lost in the Gedrosian desert, they sent him no supplies.[190] Now he summoned them to him.

Alexander greeted the Iranian satrap Astaspes warmly and confirmed him in his position, although he had sent no provisions. But Alexander soon amassed a great body of evidence of failing to send supplies and treason against Astaspes and had him arrested and executed.[191] Craterus handed over the Persians who had revolted in Arachosia. They were tried for conspiracy and executed.[192] Then the generals Cleander, Sitalces and Heraklon arrived from Media. Cleander and Sitalces were charged with plundering temples, rifling ancient tombs and high-handed treatment of their subjects. As two of the murderers of Parmenio, it was not difficult to find witnesses against them. Alexander put them to death to inspire fear in all the other satraps. Heraklon was acquitted, but soon after he was convicted of plundering the sanctuary at Susa and he too was executed.[193] Cleander's kinsman the imperial quartermaster Harpalus had more sense than to obey Alexander's summons. He fled to Athens with 5,000 talents in silver and 6,000 mercenaries.[194]

One of Alexander's most corrupt administrators – Cleomenes, who had made himself satrap of Egypt – was confirmed in his position and Philoxenus clung on in Cilicia after sending Alexander a particularly pretty boy.[195] But Alexander was still very wary of sedition and sent a letter out to his remaining satraps and generals ordering them to disband their mercenaries.[196] Only Alexander was to have the backing of troops.

News came that Nearchus had been sighted. Alexander had long since believed the fleet had been lost and had the provincial governor who reported the sighting arrested. Then Nearchus arrived, dressed in rags with his hair matted with brine. On seeing him Alexander jumped to the conclusion that he and his five companions were the only survivors. In fact, the fleet had crossed the Arabian Sea without serious loss. It now lay at Hormuz where it was undergoing a refit. Nearchus explained that the monsoon winds, the barren coastline, harassment by natives and a school of whales had delayed him.[197] Even though his failure to keep pace with the army had caused immense hardship for his men, Alexander accepted Nearchus's excuses and he organised games and a music festival to celebrate the return of the fleet, the conquest of India and the survival of his army in the desert.[198] As hero of the moment, Nearchus headed the procession and was showered with flowers. Alexander persuaded him to award a kiss to the winner of the singing and dancing competition – who turned out to be Alexander's favourite eunuch Bagoas.[199]

But the celebration was spoiled by a very public row between Craterus and Hephaestion, who had long been jealous rivals. The two men drew their swords and had to be separated. Alexander called Hephaestion 'a fool and a madman for not knowing that without Alexander's favour he was nothing'.[200] He was sent with the baggage train, the bulk of the army and the elephants along the coast road to Persepolis, while Alexander, Craterus, the Companion Cavalry, the light infantry and some regiments of archers would head overland to meet up with Nearchus and the fleet again at Susa.[201]

On the journey the purge continued. As they approached Pasargadae, the new satrap of Persis, a wealthy Iranian aristocrat named Orsines, sent out lavish gifts for Alexander and his friends – but nothing for Bagoas. When Orsines was informed that it might be wise to give Bagoas something too, he replied that 'he was honouring the friends of the king, not his harlots'.[202] This reached Bagoas's ears and he began to plot against Orsines. He did not have to wait long for his revenge. When Alexander and his men arrived at Pasargadae, they found that the tomb of Cyrus the Great had been desecrated. Its gold and silver had been looted and Cyrus's body had been thrown on the floor. Bagoas seized the opportunity to blame Orsines, who was arrested and hanged.

Aristobulus was left behind with precise instructions on how to restore the tomb. The coffin was to be repaired and what remained of Cyrus's body returned to it. The divan it sat on was to be fitted with new strapping and every single object that had previously been in the tomb was to be replaced with an exact replica. The door was then to be sealed up with blocks of stone and covered with a coat of plaster with the royal seal on it.[203]

While he was at Pasargadae, Alexander was visited by Atropates, the governor of Media. He brought with him a Mede named Baryaxes, whom he had arrested for wearing his cap upright in the

'Aristobulus relates that Alexander found the tomb of Cyrus, son of Cambyses, broken into and robbed, and that this act of profanation caused him much distress. The tomb was in the royal park at Pasargadae, . . . all it contained except the divan and the coffin had been removed. Even the royal remains had not escaped desecration . . . Alexander had the magians who guarded the monument arrested and put to the torture, hoping to extort from them the names of the culprits; but even under torture they were silent, neither confessing their own guilt nor accusing anybody else; so, as they could not be convicted of any sort of complicity in the crime, Alexander released them.'

ARRIAN OF NICOMEDIA[204]

royal fashion and proclaiming himself king of the Medes and Persians. Baryaxes' associates in the coup, came with him, also under arrest. They were all executed.[205]

At the end of January 324, Alexander continued on from Pasargadae. In March he reached Susa, where he finished his purge of disloyal satraps. He had the governor of Susiana, Abulites, and his son put to death for embezzlement and failing to send supplies when he was in the Gedrosia desert. When Abulites offered Alexander 3,000 talents in compensation, he had the cash thrown to his horses.

What kind of provisions do you call these? he said. It is said that Alexander then killed Abulites' son with a spear.[206]

News now reached Alexander that there had been a rebellion back home. His mother Olympias and sister Cleopatra, it was said, had raised an army against Antipater. Cleopatra had taken Macedonia and Olympias Epirus. Alexander was not fazed by this. Greece was a small province on the edge of his vast empire. His only comment was that Olympias would make a better queen; besides the Macedonians would never allow themselves to be ruled by a woman.[207] Anyway it does not seem to have been much of a rebellion. When the name of Antipater appears again in the literature, he still seems to be in charge in Greece and Macedonia.

When Nearchus arrived at Susa with the fleet, Alexander declared a holiday and began handing out decorations to his troops. Some were honoured with purple tunics. Peucestas and Leonnatus were crowned with gold wreathes for saving Alexander's life at Multan. Nearchus was given a golden crown and orders to build 700 new large galleys. Onesicritus, pilot of Alexander's flagship, Hephaestion and the other bodyguards were similarly honoured. Then Alexander set up tables with gold on them and paid off his soldiers' debts. It is said that 20,000 talents were distributed on this occasion.[208]

However, the festivities were overshadowed by the death of the Indian sage Calanus. Since leaving India, he had grown ill and weak. Rather than submit to being an invalid, he wanted to die.

Alexander tried to talk him out of it, but Calanus was obstinate. Eventually, he ordered Ptolemy to build a funeral pyre. Calanus was burned alive on it and it is said that his last words were directed at Alexander. They were prophetic. 'We shall meet again in Babylon,' he said as the flames consumed his body.

Funeral games and a drinking contest with huge cash prizes were organised in honour of Calanus. After the contest 35 of the drinkers died when they left the building and caught pneumonia. The winner, who had drunk 12 litres of undiluted wine, and six others died a few days later.

To consolidate his hold on power in Persia, Alexander arranged for some 80 of his most loyal officers to marry Persian or Median princesses, who had already been given a Greek education. Alexander himself took two wives – Achaemenid princesses from the two separate dynastic lines. One was Barsine, daughter of Darius, the

'Calanus was escorted to the pyre by a solemn procession – horses, men, soldiers in armour and people carrying all kinds of precious oils and spices to throw upon the flames; other accounts mention drinking-cups of silver and gold and kingly robes. He was too ill to walk, and a horse was provided for him; but he was incapable of mounting it, and had to be carried on a litter, upon which he lay with his head wreathed with garlands in the Indian fashion, and singing Indian songs, which his countrymen declare were hymns of praise to their gods. . . .

'At last he mounted the pyre and with due ceremony laid himself down.

All the troops were watching. Alexander could not but feel that there was a sort of indelicacy in witnessing such a spectacle – the man, after all, had been his friend; everyone else, however, felt nothing but astonishment to see Calanus give not the smallest sign of shrinking from the flames. We read in Nearchus's account of this incident that at the moment the fire was kindled there was, by Alexander's orders, an impressive salute: the bugles sounded, the troops with one accord roared out their battle-cry, and the elephants joined in with their shrill war-trumpetings.'

ARRIAN OF NICOMEDIA[209]

other Parysatis, daughter of Artaxerxes III Ochus. Hephaestion married another of Darius's daughters named Drypetis, so that the children of the two lovers would be cousins. The mass wedding was conducted in the Persian style – though dancers, actors and musicians came all the way from Greece to supply the entertainment. Alexander gave all the couples a dowry. He also gave wedding gifts to those Macedonians who had already married Asian women. They numbered over 10,000. The festivities lasted five days.

The Persianisation of Alexander's court was all the more apparent when he made Hephaestion *chiliarchos*, or grand vizier, and Ptolemy *edeatros*, or food taster – both traditional Persian court posts. Alexander now wanted to be known as 'lord of all', which was similar to the Persian royal titles of 'king of all countries' and 'king in this great earth far and wide'. Alexander had lost nearly half his Companion Cavalry in the Gedrosian desert and replaced them with Iranian horsemen. At the same time, his 30,000 new Bactrian troops, the 'Successors', turned up in Susa. The Macedonian veterans were not impressed and mocked them as the 'young war dancers'.[210]

In the spring of 324, the fleet carried Alexander up the Tigris. Along the way, he founded the port of Alexandria-in-Susiana where he settled veterans. It was later known as Charax and has been found near Al Qurnah in Iraq. His engineers removed several weirs that had been built by the Persians as a defence against an attack by ships with the aim of improving trade in the Persian Gulf.[211]

Alexander was now preparing new campaigns to add the Caspian region and the Arabian peninsula to his empire. But his army had now been in Asia for 12 years. Many of his older soldiers were no longer fit for service and had to be pensioned off. At Opis, he told them that they would be paid handsomely and sent home. This caused a near riot.[212] It was as if Alexander was telling the Macedonians that he no longer needed them and they feared that their king, who had already taken on Persian ways, would soon be commanding a wholly Persian army.[213] One Macedonian cried out: 'Go and conquer the world with your young war dancers.' 'With his father Ammon, you mean,' yelled another.[214]

Furious, Alexander leapt from the dais and strode into the crowd. He quickly identified the troublemakers and 13 men were dragged off and executed.[215] Alexander then reminded his Macedonians how his father Philip had turned them from a tribe of impoverished vagabonds unable to defend their borders into the masters of the Aegean.[216] Then he Alexander had made them masters of Asia. He told them that they were disloyal and cowardly and he ordered them to get out of his sight, then swept off into his pavilion, leaving them dumbfounded.[217]

Once again he stayed in his quarters for three days and would speak to no one. Veterans milled about outside, unsure of what to do. On the third day, he announced that he was forming a new elite corps – a Companion Cavalry, a Royal Squadron and a Guards Brigade – comprising only Persians. Commands previously held by Macedonians would also be given to Persians.[218] In Persian fashion these Iranian noblemen would be addressed as 'kinsmen'. They would no longer have to prostrate themselves and would be entitled to exchange the kiss of friendship with him.[219]

When the Macedonians heard this, they broke down. In tears, they rushed to his pavilion to beg his forgiveness. What hurt them the most, they said, was that Alexander had made the Persians his kinsmen, an honour never bestowed on a Macedonian.

But I regard you all as my kinsmen, said Alexander and exchanged kisses with all those present.[220]

To celebrate the reconciliation, Alexander held a banquet. Seated closest to him and drinking from the royal mixing bowl were the Macedonians, while the Persians were confined to an outer circle with others – Carians, Phoenicians, Egyptians, Babylonians, Dahae and Indians – seated around the edge. Alexander then offered up a prayer for future *harmony and partnership in rule* between Macedonians and Persians.[221]

It was clear from the seating arrangements what *partnership in rule* was to mean. His ageing Macedonian veterans were to be the administrators of his empire, while the Persians were to make up the bulk of the troops. Some 10,000 veteran infantrymen and 1,500 cavalry, nearly half of the Macedonians and Greeks in Asia, were demobilised and given a generous payoff. Those who wanted to return to Macedonia or Greece were to leave behind their Persian wives and concubines to prevent friction with the wives and lovers they had left at home. Their sons, he promised, would be given a proper Macedonian military training and, when they were grown, would return to Macedonia with him[222] – though it seems likely that his real plan was to use them to create a new corps, some 10,000 strong, loyal only to him to continue his conquests.[223]

Craterus was to lead the column heading home. With his departure, the last advocate of the old Macedonian values was being sent away from court for good. He was to replace Antipater as commander of the Macedonian forces in Europe. Antipater was ordered to bring reinforcements to Babylon. But he was afraid. He had had numerous disagreements with Olympias, who – whatever the truth behind the stories of her attempt to seize power – had been able to use her letters to her son to turn Alexander against him.

At the time, Persia was full of Greeks sent into exile by the regimes imposed on the city-states by Antipater. These troublemakers were a potential threat to the stability of the Persian empire and Alexander ordered them to return to Greece. A proclamation telling the Greek cities that they had to accept the returning exiles was read at the Olympic games. This caused consternation throughout Greece, as the cities did not want the dissidents back. Harpalus used the money he had taken from Persepolis to hire some of the returning exiles as mercenaries and added them to his private army.

Although Antipater and the other Greek states sought surreptitiously to build an alliance against Alexander, any association with Harpalus was too risky. When he offered his services to the

Athenians, they arrested him. But when Alexander tried to force them to hand him over, they stalled and, probably with Athenian contrivance, he managed to escape. Harpalus fled to Crete where he was assassinated, probably on the orders of Alexander.[224]

Alexander annoyed the Greeks by sending instructions that he should be made a god. But as some of the city-states had outstanding disputes with returning exiles about land seized from them, they went along with the request in the hope of improving their bargaining position. In Athens, Alexander's old adversary Demosthenes said simply: 'All right, make him the son of Zeus – and of Poseidon too, if that's what he wants.'[225]

To escape the summer heat of Opis, Alexander went to Ecbatana in the north, where he threw a prolonged festival in honour of Dionysus. Three thousand Greek performers were brought over to provide the entertainment. After a series of heavy drinking sessions Hephaestion fell ill and his doctor prescribed a plain diet and no alcohol. Hephaestion stuck to this for seven days, then, as soon as the doctor was not watching him, wolfed down a whole chicken and half a gallon of chilled wine. When Alexander came back from the stadium where he had been watching the boys' athletics, he found his most trusted friend dead.

He was inconsolable. When someone pointed out that Hephaestion's rival Craterus had been equally loyal, Alexander said: *Craterus loves the king; Hephaestion loves me for myself.*[226] Alexander lay on the body for a day and a night weeping. Then he had Hephaestion's doctor crucified and burnt down the nearby temple of Asclepius, the god of medicine. The body was embalmed and sent ahead to Babylon with a royal escort commanded by Perdiccas. A funeral pyre, five storeys high and half a mile around the base, was prepared. It was decorated with lions – again outraging Persian sensibilities because of the lion's association with Angra Mainyu – bulls, centaurs, gilded eagles and ships' prows. 'On top of all stood sirens, hollowed out and able to conceal within them persons who

View of Pella, Alexander's birth place

sang a lament in mourning for the dead,' wrote Diodorus.[227] It cost 10,000 talents. Alexander then commissioned a tomb that would have cost much, much more, had it ever been completed. No one was appointed to take Hephaestion's position as head of the Companion Cavalry. Alexander even sent to Siwah, to ask whether Hephaestion could be worshipped as a god. The oracles replied that he could not, but a hero-cult could be established in his honour.

Cleomenes built the appropriate shrines in Egypt. Oaths were sworn 'by Hephaestion' and, when stories of miracle cures came in, the oracle was ignored, and Hephaestion was worshipped as 'God Coadjutor and Saviour'. Interestingly, in the month after Hephaestion's death, Roxane became pregnant with Alexander's sole legitimate heir.[228] Alexander then went on the rampage, exterminating the Cossaean mountain tribes to the southwest of Ecbatana as 'an offering to the shade of Hephaestion'.[229]

Back in Macedonia, though, Olympias was happy at the news. She had always been fiercely jealous of her son's lover.

Death in Babylon
323

In February 323, Alexander and his men left Ecbatana for Babylon. But as he neared the city, he was warned by Chaldean seers that a great disaster would befall him if he entered the city through the eastern gate, as he would be facing the direction of the setting sun. He took their warning very seriously and tried to approach the city through the malarial swamps that lay to the west. This proved impossible and he eventually had to enter the city through the eastern gate.

Alexander had urgent business to conclude in Babylon. Envoys from the Greek states came to discuss the problem of their returning exiles.[230] Ambassadors from Carthage, Spain, Italy, Sicily and other places that feared invasion also arrived bearing gifts. But when no delegation arrived from Arabia, Alexander sent ships to reconnoitre the Arabian coastline and, in preparation for an invasion, dug a new harbour at Babylon, big enough to house 1,000 ships. When Alexander was told that the Arabs worshipped just two gods, Uranus and Dionysus, he said that he would take his place as a third as his achievements *surpassed those of Dionysus*.[231] A reconnaissance party had also been sent to the Caspian, complete with shipwrights who were told to build a war fleet there.[232] There were also plans to build a fleet in Cilicia to attack Carthage, Sicily and Italy. Alexander was even planning the construction of a military road across North Africa from Egypt to the Pillars of Hercules and the Atlantic.

His business done, Alexander quickly left Babylon before any disaster could befall him. He returned by boat through the malarial swamps to the west, but this trip was again dogged by strange,

'Alexander's end was now rapidly approaching. Another portent of what was so soon to come is mentioned by Aristobulus. While the King was engaged in incorporating in the various Macedonian units the troops which had come from Persia . . . , he happened to feel thirsty, and getting up from where he was sitting moved away and left the royal throne empty. . . . Only the guard of eunuchs was left standing round the throne. Now some fellow or other – some say a prisoner under open arrest – seeing the throne and the couches [around it] unoccupied, made his way up through the eunuchs and sat down on the throne. The eunuchs, according to some Persian custom, did not turn him off, but began to tear their clothes and beat their breasts and faces as if something dreadful had happened. Alexander was at once told, and ordered the man to be put to the torture in an endeavour to find out if what he had done was part of a prearranged plot. However, all they could get out of him was, that he acted as he did merely upon impulse. This served to strengthen the seers' forebodings of disaster.'

ARRIAN OF NICOMEDIA[234]

ominous events. A sudden gust of wind blew off Alexander's sun hat, which was decorated with a ribbon in the royal colours, blue and white. It landed in the reeds next to an ancient tomb belonging to the old kings of Assyria. When a sailor swam out to rescue it, to bring it back without getting it wet, he put it on his own head. Alexander rewarded him with a talent, then had him flogged for lese-majesty. In other accounts Alexander had the man beheaded 'in obedience to the prophecy which warned him not to leave untouched the head which had worn the diadem'.[233]

Worse was to come. During a review of his new troops, when Alexander briefly left the throne to have a drink, a Babylonian prisoner slipped by the guards and sat on it. Instead of throwing him off the royal eunuchs began to act as if they were in mourning. The man was tortured to find out whether this was part of a pre-arranged plot.

If there were plots against Alexander, they were probably being orchestrated by Antipater back in Greece. He knew that he would very likely be killed if he went to Babylon as Alexander had ordered. Instead Antipater sent his son Cassander to assess the king's state of mind. It is probable that Craterus, on his way back to Macedonia to replace Antipater, bumped into Cassander en route. The two men may have come to an understanding that Craterus would dawdle on his journey west. Certainly, by the time Alexander died, a year after they had set off home, Craterus and the veterans had got no further than Cilicia.[235]

When Cassander eventually arrived in Babylon, he made the mistake of tittering when he saw a Persian prostrate himself. Alexander leapt from his throne, seized him by the hair with both hands and beat his head against the wall. Later, when Cassander tried to rebut the accusations made against his father, Alexander threatened to kill both of them. This terrified Cassander. Years after Alexander was dead and Cassander was king of Macedonia, he still could not stop himself trembling uncontrollably at the sight of Alexander's portrait.[236]

A few days after Cassander arrived in Babylon, the embassy that Alexander had sent to Siwah returned, telling him that Hephaestion could be venerated as a hero or demi-god. This news was celebrated, as usual, with a series of banquets and drinking parties. There were other reasons to be cheerful: within a few days, the expeditionary force would leave for Arabia, and Alexander was looking forward to the first real addition to his empire in more than two years. The training of the fleet was now complete and triremes and quinqueremes (fast warships powered by three and five tiers of rowers respectively) were racing up and down the Euphrates, with golden wreaths being awarded to the winning crews. On 29 May 323, a party was given for Nearchus. Afterwards, Alexander's young friend Medius of Larisa invited him for a late drink. Alexander was given a large cup of undiluted wine, which he drank in one go, then 'shrieked aloud as if smitten by a violent blow'.[237] He was carried back to his quarters and put to bed.

The Roman Emperor Julius Caesar paying homage to the embalmed body of Alexander the Great, his great hero

The next day he had a fever and his condition rapidly declined. On 6 June he gave his ring to Perdiccas so that he could take over the administration of the empire. The news that Alexander was dying spread quickly. The Macedonian troops besieged the palace, threatening to break down the doors if they were not allowed in to see him. A second door was quickly knocked in Alexander's bedroom wall so that his men could file past him. By this time, he could do little more than move his eyes. The friends that crowded around his bedside asked who should inherit his kingdom. He said: *The strongest.*[238]

On the morning of 11 June 323, Alexander the Great died. The cause of death has been variously given as pleurisy, malaria picked up on his boat trip to the western gate of Babylon, alcoholism and the after-effects of the wound he had received in India. However, there were rumours at the time that he had been murdered. His last illness exhibits the symptoms of strychnine poisoning. Aristotle's friend Theophrastus described its use and dosage in his *Historia Plantarum*, and mentioned that the best way to disguise its bitter taste is to administer it in undiluted wine.[239] The most often mentioned conspirators were Antipater and Alexander's former tutor Aristotle. Both men, who were close friends back in Macedonia, had been appalled by Alexander's attempt to have himself deified. Alexander had murdered Aristotle's nephew Callisthenes and Aristotle himself wrote: 'No free man willingly endures such rule.'[240] Antipater had already been deposed as regent of Macedonia and Greece (though Craterus had yet to arrive to take power), and risked death if Alexander got his hands on him.

It is thought that Aristotle supplied the poison, which was carried to Babylon by Antipater's son Cassander in a mule's hoof. Craterus and Perdiccas would also have had to participate in the coup d'état. Certainly there were few who mourned the passing of the man they had come to see as an increasingly unpredictable tyrant. When the Athenian orator Demades heard the news, he said: 'Alexander dead? Impossible. The whole earth would stink of his corpse.'[241]

'For when Perdiccas found among the king's memoranda plans for the completion of Hephaestion's funeral monument, a very expensive project, as well as the king's other numerous and ambitious plans, which involved enormous expenditure, he decided that it was most advantageous to have them cancelled. So as not to give the impression that he was personally responsible for detracting from the king's glory, he submitted the decision on the matter to the common assembly of the Macedonians.

The following were the largest and most remarkable of the plans.

- It was intended to build 1,000 warships larger than triremes in Phoenicia, Syria, Cilicia and Cyprus for the expedition against the Carthaginians and the other inhabitants of the coastal area of Africa, Spain and the neighbouring coasts as far as Sicily; to build a coastal road in Africa as far as the Pillars of Heracles, and, as required by such a large expedition, to build harbours and shipyards at suitable places.

- To build six expensive temples at a cost of 315 tons of silver each (the temples just mentioned were

In 2003, new theories about the death of Alexander surfaced. Dr John Marr, director of epidemiology at the Virginia Department of Health, noted that, in Plutarch's account, as Alexander approached Babylon birds fell from the sky, dead at his feet. In 1999, birds in the Bronx Zoo fell dead shortly before an outbreak of West Nile disease in New York. Like malaria, West Nile disease is caused by a mosquito-born virus and produces symptoms identical to those exhibited by Alexander, who could have caught it in the malarial swamps to the west of the city. As West Nile kills less than 1 per cent of those who contract it, it would explain why there were no other deaths reported at the time. This theory is discounted by ex-Scotland Yard detective John Grieve as West Nile disease usually kills only the very old and very young. Alexander, though wounded, was strong and unlikely to have succumbed. A former deputy assistant commissioner of the Metropolitan Police, Grieve investigated the death of Alexander as if it were a murder case. He studied the poisons available in the ancient world and came up with one – white hellebore – which causes the same symptoms Alexander suffered. It has a distinctive bitter taste, which Alexander would have been sure to recognise. But it was also used as a medicine in ancient times. Grieve believes that Alexander, weakened by the wounds he had sustained on his campaigns and excessive alcohol, demoralised by the death of his lover Hephaestion and eager to get on with the invasion of the Arabian peninsula, urged his doctors to over-prescribe. This would accord with Alexander's risk-taking personality. According to Grieve, in the Macedonian culture of machismo, if Alexander had been murdered, he would have been stabbed to death like his father. With Alexander dead, his generals met to choose a new king. Perdiccas said that it was best to wait until Roxane gave birth. If she had a son, he should be the new king. But this would allow Perdiccas to rule as regent until the boy had grown up. Nearchus proposed Heracles, Alexander's three-year-old son by his concubine Barsine. But Nearchus was

to be built at Delos, Delphi and Dodona, and in Macedonia there was to be a temple of Zeus at Dium, one of Artemis Tauropolus at Amphipolis, and at Cyrnus one of Athena).

- In addition, to settle cities and transplant populations from Asia to Europe and vice versa from Europe to Asia, to bring the largest continents through intermarriage and ties of kinship to a common harmony and feeling of friendship.

- Likewise there was to be built at Troy a temple of Athena which could never be excelled in size by any other.

- A tomb for his father Philip was to be constructed which would be as large as the greatest pyramids in Egypt, which some reckon among the seven wonders of the world.

When these plans had been read out, the Macedonians, although they approved highly of Alexander, nevertheless saw that the plans were extravagant and difficult to achieve, and they decided not to carry out any of those that have been mentioned.'

DIODORUS OF SICILY[242]

married to Barsine's daughter and this would have made Nearchus unduly influential. Ptolemy objected to both these suggestions as the offspring of Roxane and Barsine were half-Persian and unfit to be king of Macedonia.

It was suggested that, as Alexander had handed Perdiccas his ring, Perdiccas himself should take the throne. But Perdiccas hesitated. Fearing that such indecisiveness would result in civil war, Meleager, commander of the phalanx, backed the candidacy of Alexander's mentally deficient illegitimate half-brother Arridaeus (with himself really in charge). Son of Philip II, Arridaeus was a full-blooded Macedonian and the phalanx hailed him as Philip III. But this caused conflict between the infantry, on the side of Meleager, and the cavalry, on the side of Perdiccas. As a result Meleager became regent for Arridaeus and Perdiccas for Roxane's son, Alexander, who was born shortly afterwards.

When the Athenians heard that Alexander had died, they revolted. Joined by several other Greek city-states, the Athenians occupied the pass of Thermopylae, cutting off the Macedonians from southern Greece. Antipater (Craterus had still not arrived to relieve him of his rule) attacked the Greek forces but was repelled and besieged in the nearby fortress of Lamia. Leonnatus came to relieve him in the spring of 322. Although Leonnatus died in the action, Antipater continued the war.

In the summer, Craterus finally arrived with 11,500 veterans on board the first ships of the new navy being built in Cilicia. He ended Athenian democracy and subjected the whole of Greece to Macedonian rule. Greeks in the east then revolted. Peithon, now satrap of Media, put down the rebellion but all this infighting had weakened the Europeans' grip on their empire and, by 316, the Indian king Chandragupta had retaken the Indus valley.

Perdiccas was occupied in Cappadocia, central Turkey, which Alexander had never conquered completely. The Macedonian satrap of neighbouring Phrygia, Antigonus Monophthalmus –

'one eye' – gave him no help. When summoned by Perdiccas to a military court to explain himself, he fled to Antipater's court in Macedonia.

At the time, Perdiccas was engaged to Antipater's daughter Nicaea, but the regent broke the engagement when Alexander's mother Olympias offered him her daughter Cleopatra, Alexander's sister and the widow of King Alexander of Epirus. If Perdiccas married a daughter of Philip, their son would have a strong claim on the throne, as Arridaeus was illegitimate and Roxane's son Alexander was half Persian. As a result, Antipater and Craterus turned against Perdiccas. Towards the end of 322, the whole confused situation descended into civil war, and Ptolemy, now the satrap of Egypt, joined in the fighting, sending his friend Ophellas to the west to conquer the Greek towns of Cyrenaica.

In December 322, Perdiccas sent the remains of Alexander to Macedonia's ancient religious capital, Aegae, where a tomb had

Oil lamp with schematised view of Alexander's tomb. Graeco-Roman Museum, Alexandria, Egypt

been prepared. But when the convoy reached Damascus, Ptolemy managed to convince its leader that Alexander had wanted to be buried in the temple of his heavenly father Zeus Ammon in Alexandria. So Alexander's corpse was taken to Egypt, where it was interred in a golden coffin.

In 321, the rebels cemented their alliance against Perdiccas by intermarriage. Antipater gave his daughters Phila and Euridice to Craterus and Ptolemy, and Nicaea, who had been promised to Perdiccas, married Lysimachus, the governor of Thrace. Perdiccas responded by sending an army under Eumenes, now the satrap of Cappadocia, against Craterus. Craterus died in the ensuing battle but the remains of his army fled the battlefield to rejoin Antipater.

Perdiccas himself marched on Egypt, arriving in May 320. Twice he tried to cross the Nile near Pelusium, but Ptolemy repulsed him. He tried crossing again near Heliopolis, but the river was high so many of his men were swept away. The rest revolted. His lieutenants Peithon, the satrap of Media, Antigenes and Seleucus, the commander of the regiment of the Shield Bearers, then turned on Perdiccas and killed him, ending the civil war.

Antipater now took over as regent for both Alexander IV and Philip III and took them, along with Roxane, back to Macedonia. The rest of the empire was divided up between Perdiccas's murderers and other allies. The death of Antipater in 319 sparked a series of wars to reunite Alexander's empire, but ended with it being broken irrevocably into its constituent parts. Antipater's successor Polyperchon invited Olympias to act as regent for Alexander IV. She refused. But in 317, when Antipater's son Cassander put Philip III on the throne, Olympias staged a coup. She killed Philip, his wife, Cassander's brother and hundreds of Cassander's followers. Cassander caught up with Olympias the following year. She was condemned to death. Cassander's men refused to carry out the sentence, but she was eventually killed by relatives of those she had executed. Then in 310, Antipater's son Cassander murdered Roxane and the 13-year-old Alexander IV. With that Alexander's direct line died out.[243] The only lasting political legacy of Alexander's empire was the Seleucid dynasty in Persia, descendants of Perdiccas's murderer Seleucus, and the Ptolemaic dynasty in Egypt, descendants of Ptolemy.

Alexander was widely damned as a tyrant in the centuries after his death. In the Book of Daniel in the Bible he is portrayed as 'The Third Beast' who unleashes a bloody tide on mankind and in the Koran as 'The Two-Horned One' who will ravage the earth with Satan in the last days. However his friend and biographer Aristobulus introduced the idea that he was driven by *pothos* or longing, that he thirsted for wisdom and longed to go beyond what had been done before.

Three hundred years after his death, when Caesar Augustus brought the idea of world conquest back into vogue, Alexander came to be seen as a demi-god. The first-century Greek writer Plutarch of Chaeronea, one of the founders of biography, portrayed him as the greatest civiliser in world history. This is his glowing assessment:

'But if you consider the effects of Alexander's instruction, you will see that he educated the Hyrcanians to contract marriages, taught the Arachosians to till the soil, and persuaded the Soghdians to support their parents, not to kill them, and the Persians to respect their mothers, not to marry them. Most admirable philosophy, which induced the Indians to worship Greek gods, and the Scythians to bury their dead and not to eat them!

'We admire the power of [the Athenian philosopher] Carneades, who caused Clitomachus, formerly called Hasdrubal and a Carthaginian by birth, to adopt Greek ways. We admire the character of [the philosopher] Zeno [of Citium], who persuaded Diogenes the Babylonian to turn to philosophy. Yet when Alexander was taming Asia, Homer became widely read, and the children of the Persians, of the Susianians and the Gedrosians sang the tragedies of Euripides and Sophocles.

'And Socrates was condemned by the sycophants in Athens for introducing new deities, while thanks to Alexander Bactria and the Caucasus worshipped the gods of the Greeks. Plato drew up in writing one ideal constitution but could not persuade anyone to adopt it because of its severity, while Alexander founded over 70 cities among barbarian tribes, sprinkled Greek institutions all over Asia, and so overcame its wild and savage manner of living. Few of us read Plato's Laws, but the laws of Alexander have been and are still used by millions of men.

'Those who were subdued by Alexander are more fortunate than those who escaped him, for the latter had no one to rescue them from their wretched life, while the victorious Alexander compelled the former to enjoy a better existence . . . Alexander's victims would not have been civilised if they had not been defeated. Egypt would not have had its Alexandria, nor Mesopotamia its Seleucia, nor Soghdiana its Prophthasia, nor India its Bucephalia, nor the Caucasus a Greek city nearby; their foundation extinguished barbarism, and custom changed the worse into better.

'If, therefore, philosophers take the greatest pride in taming and correcting the fierce and untutored elements of men's character, and if Alexander has been shown to have changed the brutish customs of countless nations, then it would be justifiable to regard him as a very great philosopher.

'Furthermore, the much-admired Republic of Zeno, the founder of the Stoic school, is built around one guiding principle: we should not live in separate cities and villages, each using its own rules of justice, but we should consider all men to be fellow-villagers and citizens, with one common life and order for all, like a flock feeding together in a common pasture. This Zeno wrote, conjuring up as it were a dream or an image of a well-ordered and philosophic constitution, but it was Alexander who turned this idea into reality. For he did not follow the advice of Aristotle and treat the Greeks as a leader would but the barbarians as a master, nor did he show care for the Greeks as friends and kinsmen, while treating the others as animals or plants; this would have filled his realm with many wars and exiles and festering unrest. Rather, believing that he had come as a god-sent governor and mediator of the whole world, he overcame by arms those he could not bring over by persuasion and brought men together from all over the world, mixing together, as it were, in a loving-cup their lives, customs, marriages and ways of living.'[244]

Alexander continued as a figure of romance throughout the Middle Ages. During the 19th century, Alexander was praised by the imperialists of the day while his father Philip was the darling of nationalists. With the founding of the League of Nations after World War One, some even saw a spark of idealism in him – the banquet at Opis was seen as an attempt to found a brotherhood of man.

However, after World War Two, when imperialism and nationalism fell distinctly out of fashion again, Alexander was seen once more as a bloodthirsty megalomaniac who ravaged an entire continent for his own personal glory. With the single exception of the founding of Alexandria, nothing significant he did survived. But his legend lives on. By his own standard of invasion and conquest, no one can match him. When the Roman Emperor Trajan reached the Persian Gulf in AD115, he wept because, at 62, he was too old to repeat Alexander the Great's feat and go on to conquer India. Alexander had reached the Gulf at the age of 25. He was dead at 32, after conquering most of the known

'He instructed all men to consider the inhabited world to be their native land, and his camp to be their acropolis and their defence, while they should regard as kinsmen all good men, and the wicked as strangers. The difference between Greeks and barbarians was not a matter of cloak or shield, or of a dagger or Median dress. What distinguished Greekness was excellence, while wickedness was the mark of the barbarian; clothing, food, marriage and way of life they should all regard as common, being blended together by ties of blood and the bearing of children.'

PLUTARCH OF CHAERONEA[245]

Sculpted portrait head of Alexander the Great as a benign deity. It has been suggested that the curled hair at his forehead alludes to the curved horns of the god Ammon. Graeco-Roman Museum, Alexandria, Egypt

world. By that age, Julius Caesar was still a lowly quaestor or magistrate, Genghis Khan was not known outside Mon-golia, and Hitler had yet to be jailed for his Beer Hall Putsch.

Although he was usually outnumbered, Alexander never lost a battle. Two millennia after his death his tactics were still being emulated. His inspired and original plan of attack at the battle of Gaugamela was reused by the Duke of Marlborough at Blen-heim in 1704 and by Napoleon at Austerlitz in 1805.[246] He was also studied by the men who developed the tank tactics used in World War Two.[247] He is still recognised as one of the greatest generals – perhaps the greatest general – of all time.

Notes

1   Peter Green, *Alexander of Macedon 356–323BC: A Historical Biography* (Berkeley: 1991) p XXXIII

2   Plutarch of Chaeronea, *Plutarch's Lives Vol 7* (London: 1919) Alexander, sections 2-3

3   Justin, *Epitome of the Philipic History of Pompeius Trogus* (Oxford: 1997) section 12.6

4   Plutarch, "Alexander", 6

5   Green, *Alexander*, p 81

6   Plutarch, "Alexander", 5

7   Aristotle, *Politics* (Cambridge: 1988) 1252b5, 1252b19

8   Athenaeus, *The Deipnosophists* (London: 1930) book 10 section 435a

9   Diodorus of Sicily, *World History* (London: 1947) book 16 section 85.5-86

10 Marcus Junianus Justinus, *Excerpt of the History of Philip by Pompeius Trogus* (Paris: 1936) section 9.5

11 Diodorus, *World History,* 17.5.3-6.3

12 Plutarch, "Alexander", 9.3

13 Green*, Alexander*, p 89

14 Robin Lane Fox, *Alexander the Great* (London: 1973) p 21

15 Lane Fox, p 23

16 Pausanias, *Description of Greece* (London: 1918) book 8 section 7.7; Justin, *Philip* 9.7.12; Plutarch, Alexander, 10.4

17 Green, *Alexander*, p 109; Lane Fox, *Alexander*, pp 23-24

18 Diodorus, *World History* 1.17.9, 1.25.3ff, 17.48.2; Plutarch, Alexander, 20.1; Quintus Curtius Rufus, *History of Alexander* (London: 1946) book 3 section 11.18

19 Plutarch, "Alexander", 14.2-3

20 Plutarch, "Alexander", 14.4; Diodorus, *World History,* 17.93.4

21 Plutarch, "Alexander", 10.6-11

22 Green, *Alexander,* p 156

23 Diodorus, *World History,* 17.7.1-3, 8-10

24 Diodorus, *World History,* 17.7.1-10

25 Arrian, *Anabasis of Alexander* (London: 1976) section 1.11.7-8; Plutarch, Alexander, 15; Plutarch, *Moralia* (London: 1936) section 331D; Diodorus, *World History,* 17.7.3; Justin, *Epitome,* 11.5.5-12

26 Arrian, *Indica* (London: 1983) 18.3

27 Diogenes Laertius, *Lives, Teachings and Sayings of Famous Philosophers* (London: 1925) book 5 section 22

28 Green, *Alexander*, p 175

29 Plutarch, "Alexander", 16

30 Arrian, *Anabasis,* 1.17.1-2

31 Green, *Alexander*, pp 199-200

32 Polynaenus, *Stratagems of War* (London: 1793) book 5 chapter 35; Arrian, *Anabasis* 3.6.6

33 Plutarch, "Alexander", 17.4; Strabo, *Geography*, (London: 1917) book 14 section 3.9

34 Plutarch, "Alexander", 18.2-3

35 Green, *Alexander*, p 214

36 Plutarch, "Alexander", 19

37 Arrian, *Anabasis,* 2.1.3-2.2.5; Quintus, *Alexander,* 3.2; Diodorus, *World History,* 17.30, 31.1-2

38 Ulrich Wilcken, *Alexander the Great* (New York: 1967) p 103

39 Green, *Alexander*, p 231

40 Lane Fox, *Alexander,* p 175

41 Quintus, *Alexander,* 3.12.15-26; Diodorus, *World History,* 17.37.5-38.7; Arrian, *Anabasis,* 2.12.6-8

42 Plutarch, "Alexander" 20-21

43 Green, *Alexander*, p 287

44 Diodorus, *World History,* 17.54.1-6; Quintus, *Alexander,* 4.11

45 Arrian, *Anabasis* 2.14

46 Plutarch, "Alexander", 20-21

47 Quintus, *Alexander,* 4.2.15

48 Quintus, *Alexander,* 4.2.10; Arrian, *Anabasis,* 2.18.1-2; Plutarch, "Alexander", 24.3

49 Quintus, *Alexander,* 4.4.10-21

50 Green, *Alexander*, p 262

51 Quintus, *Alexander,* 4.6.26-29

52 Green, *Alexander*, p 269

53 Lane Fox, *Alexander,* p 196

54 Green, *Alexander*, p 269

55 Green, *Alexander*, p 270

56 Homer, *The Odyssey* (London: 1988) book 4 lines 354-355

57 Plutarch, "Alexander", 26.3-10

58 Arrian, *Anabasis,* 3.3-4

59 Quintus, *Alexander,* 4.13.16-17; Plutarch, Alexander, 31.2-8; Diodorus, *World History,* 17.56.1

60 Quintus, *Alexander,* 4.13.23-4; E W Marsden, *The Campaign of Gaugamela* (Liverpool: 1964) p 9; Plutarch, Alexander, 32.2; Diodorus, *World History,* 17.56.1

61 Marsden, *Gaugamela*, Chapter III and references cited there

62 Marsden, *Gaugamela*, p 64

63 Green, *Alexander*, p 290

64 Green, *Alexander*, p 292

65 The Astronomical Diary of the Esagila temple complex now kept in the British Museum, see A K Grayson, *Assyrian and Babylonian Chronicles* (Locust Valley, New York: 1975) chronicle 8

66 Quintus, *Alexander,* 5.1.17-33

67 Michael Wood, *In the Footsteps of Alexander the Great*, (London: 1997) p 94

68 Quintus, *Alexander,* 5.1.36-38

69 Lane Fox, *Alexander*, p 248

70 Diodorus, *World History,* 17.69; Quintus, *Alexander,* 5.6.1-10; Justin, *Epitome,* 11.14.11-12; numbers given variously as 800 and 4,000

71 Green, *Alexander*, pp 311-2

72 Green, *Alexander*, p 315

73 Diodorus, *World History,* 17.70-71; Plutarch, Alexander, 37.1-2; Quintus, *Alexander,* 5.6.1-10; Justin, *Epitome,* 11.14.10; Strabo, *Geography*, 15.3.9

74 Plutarch of Chaeronea, *Plutarch's Lives Vol 11* (London: 1926) Artaxerxes, section 3.1

75 Arrian, *Anabasis,* 29.1-11

76 Diodorus, *World History,* 17.72; Plutarch, Alexander, 38; Quintus, *Alexander,* 5.7.1-11; Strabo, *Geography*, 15.3.6

77 Arrian, *Anabasis,* 3.19.5-8; Plutarch, Alexander, 42.3, Quintus, *Alexander,* 6.2.10; Diodorus, *World History*, 17.74.3-5; Justin, *Epitome,* 12.1.1

78 *Babylonian Chronicle* 8

79 Arrian, *Anabasis,* 3.19.5, 3.20-22.2; Quintus, *Alexander,* 5.10-13.25; Plutarch, Alexander, 42-3, *Moralia.* 332F; Justin, *Epitome,* 11.15; Diodorus, *World History,* 17.73.2-4

80   Arian, *Anabasis*, 3.21.6-22.2

81   Green, *Alexander*, p 330

82   Diodorus, *World History*, 17.76.3-8; Quintus, *Alexander*, 6.5.11-21; Arrian, *Anabasis*, 3.24.1-3, 5.19.4-6; Plutarch, "Alexander", 44.2-3, 45.3, *Moralia*, 341B

83   Quintus, *Alexander*, 6.5.23; Plutarch, "Alexander", 67

84   Plutarch, "Alexander", 22; *Moralia*. 65F, 717F

85   *Book of Arda Viraf* (London: 1872) 1.9

86   S K Eddy, *The King is Dead – Studies in the Near East Resistance to Hellenism, 334-331BC* (Lincoln, Nebraska: 1961) pp 12-19

87   Michael Wood, *In the Footsteps of Alexander*, p 96

88   Quintus, *Alexander*, 6.7.23-8; Diodorus, *World History*, 17.79.4

89   Quintus, *Alexander*, 6.7.29-30; Diodorus, *World History*, 17.79.6; Plutarch, Alexander, 49.4

90   Green, *Alexander*, p 344

91   Quintus, *Alexander*, 6.8.23-6.11.40; Plutarch, "Alexander", 49.6-7; Diodorus, *World History*, 17.80.2

92   Quintus, *Alexander*, 6.8.1-14

93   Diodorus, *World History*, 17.80.2; Quintus, *Alexander*, 7.1.5-9

94   Plutarch, *Moralia*, 183F1

95   Justin, *Epitome*, 12.5.4-8

96   Quintus, *Alexander*, 7.4.20-25

97   Quintus, *Alexander*, 7.5.1-16

98   Green, *Alexander*, p 357

99   Green, *Alexander*, p 363

100 Arrian, *Anabasis*, 2.19.1-5; Diodorus, *World History*, 17.42.1-2; Quintus, *Alexander*, 4.2.24, 3.2-5

101 Arrian, *Anabasis*, 2.19.6-20.2.3; Quintus, *Alexander*, 4.3.1; Plutarch, "Alexander", 24.2

102 Quintus, *Alexander*, 8.3.1

103 Green, *Alexander*, p 367

104 Arrian, *Anabasis*, 4.18.4-19.6

105 Lucian of Samosata, *Paintings*, section 7

106 Arrian, *Anabasis*, 4.21, 4.22.1-2; Strabo, *Geography*, 11.11.4

107 Quintus, *Alexander*, 8.5.1; Arrian, *Anabasis*, 4.22.3, 7.6.1; Diodorus, *World History*, 17.108.1-3; Plutarch, "Alexander", 47.3, 71.1

108 Herodotus, *Histories*, 1.134

109 Arrian, *Anabasis*, 4.10.5-12.5

110 Quintus, *Alexander,* 8.6-8, 8.8.15, 8.8.19-23; Arrian, *Anabasis,* 4.13-14; Plutarch, "Alexander", 55.2-5; Stabo, *Geography,* 11.11.4

111 Quintus, *Alexander,* 7.10.11-12; Arrian, *Anabasis,* 4.7.1-5, 4.15.1-6; Strabo, *Geography,* 11.7.4

112 Diodorus, *World History,* 2.38.3.63, 4.3; Arrian, *Anabasis,* 8.5, 8.8-9

113 Quintus, *Alexander,* 8.8.15

114 Ktesias, *Ancient India* (London: 1882) p 15, 63

115 Arrian, *Anabasis,* 5.1.1-2.2

116 Philostratus, *Life of Apollonius of Tyana* (London: 1912) section 2.8

117 Arrian, *Anabasis,* 5.10. 1-2

118 Quintus, *Alexander,* 8.12.10-18; Arrian, *Anabasis,* 5.8.1-2; Plutarch, Alexander, 59.1-3

119 Arrian, *Anabasis,* 5.8.2-3; Quintus, *Alexander,* 8.13.1-5

120 Arrian, *Anabasis,* 6.1.2, 6.1.5

121 Arrian, *Anabasis,* 7.1.5-3.6

122 Strabo, *Geography,* 15.1.61, 62-64

123 Arrian, *Anabasis,* 7.1.5-3.6

124 Strabo, *Geography,* 15.1.61, 62-64

125 Strabo, *Geography,* 15.1.61, 62-64

126 Arrian, *Anabasis,* 5.8.2-3, 5.15.4; Diodorus, *World History,* 17.87.2; Quintus, *Alexander,* 8.13.1-5, 8,13.6

127 J F C Fuller, *The Generalship of Alexander the Great* (London: 1958) p 181

128 Quintus, *Alexander,* 8.13.6, 8-9, 10-11; Arrian, *Anabasis,* 5.9.1, 3-4

129 Arrian, *Anabasis,* 5.9.2-3; Quintus, *Alexander,* 8.13.12-16; Plutarch, "Alexander", 60.1-2

130 Arrian, *Anabasis,* 5.11.1-2; Quintus, *Alexander,* 8.13.17; Frontinus, *The Stratagems* (London: 1925) book 1 section 4.9

131 Arrian, *Anabasis,* 5.10.3-4; Quintus, *Alexander,* 8.13.17-19

132 Diodorus, *World History,* 17.87.3

133 Green, *Alexander,* p 392

134 Quintus, *Alexander,* 8.13.20-21

135 Arrian, *Anabasis,* 5.12.1; Fuller, *Generalship,* pp 186-7

136 Arrian, *Anabasis,* 5.11.3-4

137 Fuller, *Generalship,* pp 188-90

138 Arrian, *Anabasis,* 5.12.2-13.3; Quintus, *Alexander,* 8.13.22-7; Plutarch, "Alexander", 60.2-4

139 Quintus, *Alexander,* 8.14.1-2

140 Arrian, *Anabasis,* 5.13.4; Plutarch, "Alexander", 60.4

141 Arrian, *Anabasis,* 5.14.1-6; Quintus, *Alexander,* 8.14.1-8; Plutarch, "Alexander", 60.5; Justin, *Epitome,* 12.7.4

142 Green, *Alexander*, p 396

143 Arrian, *Anabasis,* 5.15.4-7; Diodorus, *World History,* 17.87.4-5; Quintus, *Alexander,* 8.14.10-13

144 Arrian, *Anabasis,* 5.16.1-4, 5.17.1-3; Quintus, *Alexander,* 8.14.14-15, 18; Plutarch, "Alexander", 60.5

145 Arrian, *Anabasis,* 5.17.3; Quintus, *Alexander,* 8.14.19

146 Arrian, *Anabasis,* 5.17.3-5; Diodorus, *World History,* 17.88.1-2

147 Arrian, *Anabasis,* 5.17.7

148 Arrian, *Anabasis,* 5.17.6-7; Diodorus, *World History,* 17.88.2-6; Quintus, *Alexander,* 8.14.22-29; Plutarch, "Alexander", 60.6.

149 Arrian, *Anabasis,* 5.18.1-3; Diodorus, *World History,* 17.89.1-3

150 Arrian, *Anabasis,* 5.18.4-19.3 (quote 19.1)

151 Arrian, *Anabasis,* 5.18.3 (5.14.1, 5.12.2); Diodorus, *World History,* 17.89.3

152 Green, *Alexander*, p 401

153 Aristotle, *Meteorologica* (London: 1952) 2.5, 362B 20-29

154 Arrian, *Anabasis,* 5.20.8-5.24.8; Diodorus, *World History,* 17.90-02; Quintus, *Alexander,* 9.1.14-35; Strabo, *Geography*, 15.1.30-31

155 Arrian, *Anabasis,* 5.24.5

156 H G Rawlinson, *India: A Short History* (London: 1938) p 60

157 Diodorus, *World History,* 17.93.2; Plutarch, "Alexander", 62.2

158 A V Williams-Jackson, *Cambridge History of India* (Cambridge: 1922) vol I, p 341; W W Tarn, *Alexander the Great* (Cambridge: 1948) vol I, p 98, vol II, p 284

159 Quintus, *Alexander,* 9.2.10-11; Diodorus, *World History,* 17.94.1-5

160 Arrian, *Anabasis,* 5.27.1-9; Quintus, *Alexander,* 9.2.31-9.3.15; Justin, *Epitome,* 12.8.10-15

161 Arrian, *Anabasis,* 5.28.1-3; Plutarch, "Alexander", 62.3; Quintus, *Alexander,* 9.3.16-18

162 Arrian, *Anabasis,* 5.28.1-3; Plutarch, "Alexander", 62.3; Quintus, *Alexander,* 9.3.16-18

163 Arrian, *Anabasis,* 5.28.1-29.1

164 Arrian, *Anabasis,* 5.29.1-2; Diodorus, *World History,* 17.95.1-2; Quintus, *Alexander,* 9.3.19; Plutarch, Alexander, 62.4; Justin, *Epitome,* 12.8.16-17

165 Philostratus, *Life of Apollonius,* 2.43

166 Quintus, *Alexander* 9.3.21-22; Diodorus, *World History* 17.95.3-4

167 Pliny, *Natural History* (London: 1938) book 16 section 62.144

168 Plutarch, "Alexander", 35.8; Diodorus, *World History,* 17.108.5-6; Tarn, *Alexander*, vol I, p 131

169 Plutarch, "Alexander", 41.4

170 Green, *Alexander*, p 417

171 Arrian, *Anabasis* 6.4.4-6.5.4; Diodorus, *World History,* 17.97; Quintus, *Alexander,* 9.4.8-14; Plutarch, "Alexander", 58.4

172 Diodorus, *World History,* 17.98.1-2; Quintus, *Alexander,* 9.4.15

173 Quintus, *Alexander,* 9.4.16-23

174 Arrian, *Anabasis,* 6.5.5-6.6.5

175 Arrian, *Anabasis,* 6.6.6-6.7.6; Tarn, *Alexander*, vol I, p 103

176 Quintus, *Alexander,* 9.4.27-30

177 Arrian, *Anabasis,* 6.9.11; Diodorus, *World History,* 17.98.3-99.4; Quintus, *Alexander,* 9.4.26-9.5.18; Plutarch, "Alexander", 63.1-4; Justin, *Epitome,* 12.9.5-11; Plutarch, *Moralia,* 327B, 343D-344D

178 Quintus, *Alexander,* 9.5.22-30; Plutarch, "Alexander", 63.5-6; Justin, *Epitome,* 12.9.12-13; Plutarch, *Moralia*, 344F-345B

179 Arrian, *Anabasis,* 6.12.22

180 Quintus, *Alexander,* 9.7.1-11; Diodorus, *World History,* 17.99.5-6

181 Arrian, *Anabasis,* 6.12-14.3; Plutarch, "Alexander", 63.5-6; Justin, *Epitome,* 12.9.12-13; Plutarch, *Moralia*, 344F-345B

182 Diodorus, *World History,* 17.100-101; Quintus, *Alexander,* 9.7.15-26

183 Arrian, *Anabasis,* 6.14.4-6.17.2; Diodorus, *World History,* 17.100-102; Quintus, *Alexander,* 9.8.3-16; Plutarch, "Alexander", 59.4, 64

184 Arrian, *Anabasis,* 6.24.3

185 Arrian, *Anabasis,* 6.20.5

186 Plutarch of Chaeronea, *Plutarch's Lives Vol 8* (London: 1919) Eumenes, section 2.2-3

187 Arrian, *Anabasis,* 6.26.3

188 Green, *Alexander*, p 435

189 Quintus, *Alexander,* 8.10.15-18

190 Plutarch, "Alexander", 68.3

191 Green, *Alexander*, p 438

192 Nicholas G L Hammond, *Alexander the Great* (London: 1981) p 242

193 Arrian, *Anabasis,* 6.27.3-5

194 Diodorus, *World History,* 17.108.5-8

195 Plutarch, "Alexander", 22 and *Moralia,* 333A, 1099D

196 Diodorus, *World History,* 17.106.3

197 Arrian, *Anabasis,* 6.27.3, 8.21, 8.36.3-4; Quintus, *Alexander*, 10.1.9; Strabo, *Geography*, 15.2.5, 11; Diodorus, *World History*, 17.104.3-6, 106.6-7; Plutarch, *Alexander*, 47.5-6, 67.3-4 and *Moralia*, 337A

198 Arrian, *Anabasis,* 6.28.3

199 Plutarch, "Alexander", 67.3-4; Arrian, *Anabasis,* 6.28.3, 8.36.3-4; Diodorus, *World History,* 17.106.4-6

200 Plutarch, "Alexander", 47.6

201 Arrian, *Anabasis,* 6.28.7-29.1; 8.36-37.1; Diodorus, *World History,* 17.107.1

202 Quintus, *Alexander,* 10.1.26

203 Arrian, *Anabasis,* 29.1-11

204 Arrian, *Anabasis,* 29.1-11

205 Arrian, *Anabasis,* 29.1-11

206 Arrian, *Anabasis,* 6.30.1-7.4.3; Plutarch, "Alexander", 68.1-4; Diodorus, *World History,* 17.106.4; Quintus, *Alexander,* 10.1.17-19

207 Arrian, *Anabasis,* 7.6; Diodorus, *World History,* 17.108.1-3; Plutarch, "Alexander", 68.2-3 71.1-2; Justin, *Epitome,* 12.11.4-5; Quintus, *Alexander,* 10.1.43-5

208 Arrian, *Anabasis,* 7.4.4-5.6

209 Arrian, *Anabasis,* 7.1.5-3.6

210 Diodorus, *World History,* 17.108.3; Arrian, *Anabasis,* 7.6.4-5

211 Arrian, *Anabasis,* 7.7.1-7; Strabo, *Geography*, 16.1.9

212 Arrian, *Anabasis,* 7.8-11.7; Plutarch, "Alexander", 71.2-4; Justin, *Epitome,* 12.11.4-12.12.7; Diodorus, *World History,* 17.108.3, 109.2-3; Quintus, *Alexander,* 10.2.12-10.3.14

213 Arrian, *Anabasis,* 7.8.2; Diodorus, *World History,* 17.108.3, 109.2; Plutarch, "Alexander", 71.2; Justin, *Epitome,* 12.11.5; Quintus, *Alexander,* 10.2.12-13

214 Arrian, *Anabasis,* 7.8.3; Diodorus, *World History,* 17.109.2; Justin, *Epitome,* 12.11.6

215 Arrian, *Anabasis,* 7.8.3; Diodorus, *World History,* 17.109.2; Justin, *Epitome,* 12.11.7-8; Quintus, *Alexander,* 10.2.30, 10.4.2-3

216 Arrian, *Anabasis,* 7.9-10; Quintus, *Alexander,* 10.2.15-30; Plutarch, "Alexander", 71.3

217 Arrian, *Anabasis,* 7.11.2

218 Arrian, *Anabasis,* 7.11.1-2; Quintus, *Alexander,* 10.3.7-14; Diodorus, *World History,* 17.109.3; Plutarch, "Alexander". 71.3; Justin, *Epitome,* 12.12.1-4

219 Arrian, *Anabasis,* 7.11.2-3

220 Arrian, *Anabasis,* 7.11.4-7; Plutarch, "Alexander", 71.4; Diodorus, *World History,* 17.109.3; Justin, *Epitome,* 12.12.5-7

221 Arrian, *Anabasis,* 7.11, 8-9

222 Arrian, *Anabasis,* 7.12.1-2; Diodorus, *World History,* 17.110.3; Plutarch, "Alexander", 71.5

223 Green, *Alexander*, p 457

224 Green, *Alexander*, p 467

225 Plutarch, *Moralia*, 187E, 804B, 842D

226 Arrian, *Anabasis*, 7.13-14; Diodorus, *World History,* 17.110.7-8; Athenaeus, *Deiposophists*, 12.536A-B

227 Diodorus, *World History* 17.114-5

228 Justin, *Epitome*, 12.12.11-12; Plutarch, "Alexander", 47, 72, Eumenes, 1, 2.4-5, *Moralia*, 181D 29, 180D 14

229 Plutarch, "Alexander", 72.3

230 Diodorus, *World History,* 17.113.3

231 Arrian, *Anabasis,* 7.20.1

232 Green, *Alexander*, p 468

233 Arrian, *Anabasis*, 7.212-2; Diodorus, *World History*, 17.116.5-6; Strabo, *Geography*, 9.2.18

234 Arrian, *Anabasis* 7.24.1-3

235 Green, *Alexander*, p 460

236 Arrian, *Anabasis,* 7.23.2; Plutarch, "Alexander", 74;

237 Diodorus, *World History,* 17.117.2

238 Green, *Alexander*, p 475

239 R D Milne, *Alexander the Great* (London: 1968) p 256-8

240 Aristotle, *Politics*, 1295A22

241 Plutarch of Chaeronea, *Plutarch's Lives Vol 8* (London: 1919) Phocion 22

242 Diodorus, *World History,* 18.4.1-6

243 Green, *Alexander*, p 478

244 Plutarch, *Moralia,* 328C-329D

245 Plutarch, *Moralia,* 328C-329D

246 Green, *Alexander*, p 290

247 Fuller, *Generalship*, p 5; Viscount Montgomery of Alamein, *A History of Wafare* (London: 1968) pp 82-83

Chronology

Year	Age	Life
356		Born in Pella, Macedonia, on 20 or 26 July, son of Philip II of Macedonia (382-336) and his wife Olympias of Epirus (375-316).
343/2	13	Aristotle (384-322) arrives in Macedonia to become Alexander's tutor.
340	15	Alexander becomes regent of Macedonia, defeats the Maedi and founds Alexandropolis Conservatory.
338	17	Alexander distinguishes himself at the battle of Chaeronea and visits Athens as an ambassador. Philip marries Eurydice and Alexander and Olympias go into exile.
337	18	Alexander returns to Pella and the League of Corinth declares war on Persia.
336	19	Spring: Parmenio (c400-330BC) leads vanguard of Macedonians into Asia. Meanwhile Artaxerxes IV is murdered and Darius III succeeds to the throne of Persia. October: Philip II is murdered and Alexander becomes king of Macedonia. November-December: Alexander is confirmed as leader of the Persian expedition by the League of Corinth.
335	20	Summer: Alexander campaigns in the Balkans. Meanwhile the Greek mercenary Memnon, fighting for the Persians, counterattacks in Asia. Thebes rebels and Alexander destroys the city in late September.
334	21	May: Alexander lands in Asia and visits Troy. June: He defeats Memnon at the battle of the river Granicus. Summer: Miletus falls and Alexander besieges the Persians at Halicarnassus.
333	22	Winter: Alexander conquers Caria, Lycia, Pamphylia and Phrygia. March-June: Memnon begins a naval offensive in the Aegean to cut Alexander off in Asia but dies soon after. April-July: Alexander visits Gordium and cuts the Gordian knot. Darius marches west from Babylon. August: Alexander enters the Cilicia gates and reaches Tarsus where he falls ill. Recovering, he defeats Darius at the battle of Issus. Darius tries to make peace settlement.

Year	Age	Life
332	23	January: The siege of Tyre begins. Spring: The Persian fleet disintegrates. July: Tyre falls. September-October: Gaza is besieged and taken. 14 November: Alexander crowned as Pharaoh in Memphis.
331	24	February: Alexander visits the oracle of Ammon at Siwah. 7 April: Alexander founds Alexandria. May: He consolidates his position in Phoenicia and takes Syria. Late July: Alexander sets out eastwards to campaign in Mesopotamia. 1 October: Darius is defeated at the battle of Gaugamela. 21 October: Alexander enters Babylon. December: Alexander occupies Susa and his forces advance to the Persian gates.
330	25	January: Alexander takes Persepolis and sacks it. May: He burns the city down. June: Alexander reaches Ecbatana. Parmenio is left there with Harpalus as treasurer. July: Darius III is murdered and Bessus becomes 'Great King' in Bactria. August-September: Alexander takes Hyrcania, Parthia and Aria. October: Alexander marches on into Drangiana where he uncovers the 'plot of Philotas'. November: Parmenio is murdered in Ecbatana. December: Armies unite in Arachosia.
329	26	March: Alexander advances to Gandara. April-May: Alexander crosses the Hindu Kush. June: Alexander advances to the Oxus where the veterans and Thessalian volunteers are dismissed. Bessus is captured and Alexander advances to Maracanda (Samarkand). Spitamenes leads a revolt in Soghdiana and annihilates a Macedonian cavalry detachment.
328	27	Alexander winters in Bactra, then campaigns in Bactria and Soghdiana in the spring and summer. Autumn: He murders Cleitus in a drunken brawl. December: Spitamenes is defeated and executed.
327	28	Spring: Alexander captures the Soghdian Rock. He meets and marries Roxane (343-310), daughter of Soghdian nobleman Oxyartes. He introduces *proskynesis*, the Persian art of self-abasement. His pages conspire to murder him and he kills Callisthenes. Summer: Alexander recrosses the Hindu Kush and begins the invasion of India.
326	29	February: Hephaestion advances through Gandara to the Indus river. Alexander campaigns in the Swat valley and takes the Aornus rock. April: Armies unite near the Indus and advance to Taxila. May: Alexander defeats the rajah Porus at the battle of the Hydaspes. Late July: The army mutinies at the Hyphasis (Beas) river. November: Alexander's fleet starts on its homeward journey down the Hydaspes.

325	30	January: Alexander is wounded in his campaign against the Malli. June: Craterus starts out across country for Carmania. Late August: Alexander starts out down the Makran Coast. 15 September: Nearchus sets out along the coast with the fleet while Alexander crosses the Gedrosian desert. December: Alexander purges the disloyal satraps and meets Craterus in Carmania. Harpalus flees.
324	31	January: Alexander meets Nearchus in Carmania and sends the fleet on to Susa. Alexander visits Pasargadae where Cyrus the Great's tomb had been desecrated. March: Alexander meets Nearchus in Susa. Alexander's Indian adviser Calanus burns himself to death. Mass mar- riages between Macedonians and Persians are held at Susa and the Iranian 'Successors' arrive. August: Alexander issues his decree order ing Greek cities to accept their returning political exiles and the Macedonians mutiny at Opis. Their reconciliation is celebrated with a huge banquet and Alexander prays for 'harmony and partnership' between Macedonians and Persians. Then the veterans set off home with Craterus. October: Alexander moves on to Ecbatana, where Hephaestion dies.
323	32	Harpalus is assassinated on Crete. Alexander arrives at Babylon, despite ill omens. Greek states deify Alexander at his request. Alexander takes a boat-trip through malarial marshes. Antipater's son Cassander arrives at Babylon, possibly carrying poison. 29 May: Alexander falls ill after a party. 11 June: Alexander dies.

Sources and Further Reading

Although stories about Alexander appear in the literature of 80 nations, reliable sources are scant. All biographies rely on five principle sources. These begin with Diodorus, a Sicilian Greek of the 1st century BC, who wrote a universal history in 40 books, 15 of which survive. In the 1st century AD came the Latin author Quintus Curtius Rufus, who wrote *History of Alexander*, in ten books, most of which survive. In the 2nd century, Plutarch wrote his *Life of Alexander*, Justin wrote a summary of an earlier work by Pompeius Trogus, which has been lost, and Arrian wrote his *Anabasis of Alexander*. These were based on early accounts, principally the reports Callisthenes of Olynthus sent back to his uncle Aristotle until he was executed by Alexander in 325. Alexander's general and close friend Ptolemy wrote an account, much of which survives in the work of Arrian. Others wrote their memoirs and over 400 fragments from around 30 lost writers survive. Plutarch, as one of the founders of the principles of biography, is particularly good on naming his sources. Modern Alexander studies began in 1833, with the publication of a biography by Johann Gustav Droysen in Prussia where modern critical historical method was developed. Since then there have been huge advances in archaeology, papyrology, epigraphy, paleography and numismatics, all of which have helped substantiate the story of Alexander.

Arrian, *The Campaigns of Alexander* (1958; reprint, Penguin Books, Harmondsworth, 1976) – written in Athens four hundred years after Alexander's death, this remains the most reliable account of Alexander's achievements. (Also translated as *The Anabasis of Alexander*.)

Briant, Pierre, *Alexander the Great – The Heroic Ideal,* trans Jeremy Leggart (1987; Thames & Hudson, London, 2001) – accessible and fully illustrated account of the life of Alexander in Thames & Hudson's New Horizon series.

J F C Fuller, *The Generalship of Alexander the Great* (London: 1958) – one of the leading theorists of modern tank warfare gives his assessment.

Green, Peter, *Alexander of Macedon 356–323BC: A Historical Biography* (University of California Press, Berkeley, 1991) – a lively account of Alexander's life by the Dougherty Centennial Professor Emeritus of Classics at the University of Texas, Austin.

Diodorus of Sicily, *World History*, trans C H Oldfather and others (London: 1933) – the oldest existing account of the life of Alexander.

Hammond, Nicholas G L, *Alexander the Great: King, Commander and Statesman* (Chatto & Windus, London: 1981) – a balanced account of the significance of Alexander by a leading academic authority.

Justin, *Epitome of the Philippic History of Pompeius Trogus* (Oxford: 1997) – a short account, condensed from an earlier general history.

Lane Fox, Robin, *Alexander the Great* (1973; reprint, Penguin Books, Harmondsworth: 1986) – a prize-winning book that has remained in print for 30 years.

O'Brian, John Maxwell, *Alexander the Great: The Invisible Enemy* (Routledge, London: 1992) – a scholarly examination of the psychology of Alexander, written for the general reader, playing down the military and political aspects of his life.

Plutarch of Chaeronea, *Plutarch's Lives Vol 7* (London: 1919) – although writing over 400 years after the event, Plutarch is acknowledged as one of the best-read men in the ancient world.

Renault, Mary, *The Nature of Alexander* (1975; Penguin Books, Harmondsworth, 1983) – a retelling of the story of Alexander with the insight of an accomplished novelist.

Strabo, *Geography*, trans Horace Leonard Jones (London: 1917-32) – the first survey of the classical world including the histories of the countries covered.

Quintus Curtius Rufus, *The History of Alexander*, trans John Yardley (Penguin Books, Harmondsworth: 1984) – a highly readable translation of the only Latin text on Alexander of Macedonia. Originally, the History of Alexander consisted of ten books, but the first two books, covering the events between the accession of Alexander and the death of the Persian commander Memnon of Rhodes, are now missing. What remains starts with the Macedonian army's march through Phrygia in the spring of 333 and ends with the burial of Alexander's body in a golden sarcophagus in Egypt in 321.

W W Tarn, *Alexander the Great* (University Press, Cambridge: 1948) – the most famous account of Alexander's life of the modern era, though Tarn is often criticised for being too idealistic in portraying Alexander as the first to contemplate the unity of mankind.

Wilcken, Ulrich, *Alexander the Great*, trans G C Richards (W W Norton & Company, Inc, New York: 1967, originally published 1931) – a distinguished academic biography by the leading German classicist, which includes an introduction to Alexander studies by Eugene N Borza of Pennsylvania State University.

Wood, Michael, *In the Footsteps of Alexander the Great* (BBC Books, London: 1997) – published to accompany the BBC television series of the same name, the book follows Michael Wood's modern-day journey along the trail of Alexander's conquests.

Selected websites

www.livius.org/aj-al/alexander/alexander00.html
A comprehensive series of articles related to Alexander, his life, conquests and colleagues, along with a chronology of his life and picture gallery.

www.pothos.org
This is an extensive site devoted to Alexander the Great with sections on art and legends, his campaigns, his contemporaries, and books and movies about him.

www.isidore-of-seville.com/Alexanderama.html
Annotated web directory for information on the Macedonian conqueror.

www.hackneys.com/alex_web
Comprehensive information on everything from his parents to his tactics and weapons.

hum.ucalgary.ca/wheckel/alexande.htm.
The University of Calgary's authoritative site.

home.earthlink.net/~mathetria/hephaistion.html
A site dedicated to the life and career of Hephaestion, Alexander the Great's lover, best friend and general.

www.royalty.nu/Europe/Balkan/Alexander.html
Biography and annotated bibliography on Alexander and related topics.

www.e-classics.com/ALEXANDER.htm
Plutarch's life of Alexander, in an abridged modern English version.

www.alexanderthegreat.gr
This site provides a general overview which includes biography.

www.mpt.org/programsinterests/mpt/alexander
This is the companion site to BBC TV's series *In the Footsteps of Alexander the Great* with Michael Wood provided by Maryland Public Television. It includes an episode guide and stories from Wood's own journey.

ethassite.freewebsites.com/alexanderhome.html
A detailed biography and history of Alexander, entitled the 'Alexander the Great Report'.

www.trentu.ca/ahc/ch207b-bib.html
A bibliography on Alexander, including monographs, source-books and special topics, though limited to titles published in the English language.

home.earthlink.net/~mathetria/Beyond_Renault
/beyondrenault.html
A listing, with academic reviews, of 20th century fiction in all genres that features Alexander the Great.

dir.yahoo.com/Science/Biology/Zoology/Animals__Insects__and
_Pets/Mammals/Horses/Individual_Horses/Bucephalus

A site dedicated to Alexander's war horse.

www.gayheroes.com/alex.htm

This site offers evidence that Alexander was gay.

Picture Sources

The author and publishers wish to express their thanks to the following sources of illustrative material and/or permission to reproduce it. They wil make the proper acknowledgements in future editions in the event that any omissions have occured.

AKG London: pp. 15, 31. Mary Evans Picture Library: pp. 6, 12, 21, 24, 32, 35, 39, 69, 74, 89, 96, 106, 118, 136. Topham Picture Point: pp. 4, 42, 52, 56, 60, 66, 77. Werner Forman: pp. 49, 132, 141, 146.

Index

Issus, 30; probable relationship with Statira, 34; rejects Darius's terms, 34–6, 48; installed as pharaoh, 43; called 'king of the world', 58; policy of appointing Persians to office, 58, 70, 72, 129; lack of concern for money, 65; succession to Persian throne, 67–8, 82, 91; relationship with Bagoas, 69; adopts Persian ways, 69–71, 110, 128; called 'the Accursed', 70; plot against, 73, 78; moves against Parmenio, 73, 76–9; reverses policy of appointing Persians to office, 78–9; refuses food and drink, 81, 85; wounded at Cyropolis, 83; drinking, 84, 93, 122, 137, 139; accused of blasphemy, 84; kills Cleitus, 85; contemplates suicide, 85; gives soldier his seat, 87; marriage with Roxane, 88–90; introduces *proskynesis*, 91–3; injured in Himalayas, 95; generosity, 99; with Indian philosophers, 99–101; needs no reason for conquest, 111; withdraws to tent, 111–12; decides to turn back, 112; shortage of money, 113–14, 120; wounded in India,

116–18, 123, 137; marries Persian princesses, 127–8; called 'lord of all', 128; turns against Antipater, 130; and Hephaestion's death, 131, 139; journey to Babylon, 133–5; plots against, 134; taken ill, 135–7; death, 137, 140; cause of death, 137–9; interred in Alexandria, 141; line dies out, 142; reputation and legacy, 143–6

Alexander IV (son of Roxane), 140–2

Alexander sarcophagus, 52–3

'Alexanderville' (Sikandarpur), 106

Alexandria, 42–4, 97, 144–5; Alexander interred, 141

Alexandria (Iskenderun), 32

Alexandria (Kapisa), 78

Alexandria-in-Susiana, 128

Alexandria-in-the-Caucasus, 79, 97

Alexandria-of-the-Areians, 72

Alexandria-the-Furthest, 83

Alexandropolis, 7

Amanic gates, 29

Amasis, pharaoh, 45

Ambhi, 95, 98–9, 102, 108

Amminapes, 42–3, 68, 70

Ammon, 1, 5, 15, 42, 45, 129, 146; oracle, 44–6, 64

Amphipolis, 3, 139

Anatolia, 9, 23, 26

Krishna, 98

Ktesias, 94

Lade, 22

Lamia, 140

Leonidas, 9

Leonnatus, 92, 116, 122; decorated, 126; death, 140

Lesbos, 22

Leuctra, battle of, 1

Libya, 8, 44

lions, 131

Lucian of Samosata, 88

lunar month, 58

Lycia, 23

Lydia, 22

lyres, 18

Lysimachus, 142

Macedonia, 5, 41, 70, 92, 117, 132, 137; economic position, 1; royal line, 1; Philip consolidates rule, 2–3; exiles in, 3, 6, 25, 36, 90; at war with Greece, 8–9; dynasty, 11; hegemony in Greece, 13, 22, 140; at war with Persia, 23, 35, 38, 65, 67, 110–11; Antipater as regent, 24, 78, 126, 140–2; Alexander's army returns, 111–13, 130, 135; rebellion, 126; Cassander becomes king, 135; Antipater

replaced as regent, 137; commemorative temples planned for Hephaestion, 139; macho culture, 139; succession, 139–42; end of civil war, 142

Macedonian army, 1–2, 16, 84; numbers, 14, 17, 47, 50, 84, 90, 102, 104; pay, 15, 65, 87; at battle of Granicus, 18–21; casualties, 24, 32, 40, 60, 79, 84, 87, 109, 121; dancing girls tactic, 23; at battle of Issus, 29–30, 32; siege of Tyre, 38, 40; at battle of Gaugamela, 49–51, 54; reorganised, 59; desire to return home, 67–8, 111–12; garrison massacred in Aria, 72; discontent among, 72–3, 79, 91, 99, 110–12, 115; treason trials, 73; letters intercepted, 78; grievances heard, 78; endure hardships, 79–81, 86–7, 97; vulnerability, 83; training, 90, 130; in India, 95, 98; at battle of Hydaspes, 104–8; gives thanks for victory, 112; new supplies, 113; return home, 115, 117, 135; garrisons slaughtered in Punjab, 118; decorations awarded, 126; debts paid off, 126; Persian elements, 128–30,